Emperors
of Song

Emperors of Song

Three Great Impresarios

FREDDIE
STOCKDALE

JOHN MURRAY
Albemarle Street, London

First published in 1998
by John Murray (Publishers) Ltd,
50 Albemarle Street, London W1X 4BD

A catalogue record for this book is available from the British Library

ISBN 0-7195-5702 X

Typeset in Baskerville MT by Servis Filmsetting Ltd, Manchester
Printed and bound in Great Britain by
The University Press, Cambridge.

To Adele, with love

Contents

Illustrations

Illustrations

The author and publishers wish to thank the following for permission to reproduce illustrations: plate 2, Susan Foreman, *From Palace to Power: An Illustrated History of Whitehall* (Alpha Press, 1995); 4 and 11, Robert Tuggle; 6, Corbis-Bettman; 9, 13 and 15, Brown Brothers.

Introduction

I STARTED THE reading for this book with a professional interest in learning about opera's past, and ended it amazed that today's received image of presenting opera in Britain should be so very different from what prevailed for the three centuries up to the outbreak of the Second World War.

Although private (as opposed to government) enterprise alone still provides grand opera in the United States, as it did in Britain from 1637 to 1945, in Britain the post-war state-funded arrangement has fundamentally changed the market (with the single glorious exception of Glyndebourne) for the period between 1945 and 1998.

Fifty-three years of state nationalisation cannot rewrite three hundred years of opera history, however, so it is necessary first to sketch in those early years, in order to make it clear that the impresarios in this book were not engaged in some foolhardy, quixotic task of comic eccentricity, but rather in the perfectly natural British and North American entrepreneurial endeavour of presenting opera for profit. Many impresarios made their fortune in this way, a notable example being Carl Rosa, born into a poor family in 1842, who when he died in 1889 left the

I

equivalent today of more than fifteen million pounds in his Will.

There are many definitions of the word 'impresario', and many people who might claim the designation. But for the purposes of this book, I have limited myself to three essential ingredients for inclusion here. By these criteria, an impresario is, firstly, someone who acts, for the most part alone, as principal in undertaking the financing and presentation of public performances of opera. Leadership of a broad syndicate, as exemplified by Sir Augustus Harris, who presented opera intermittently at Covent Garden at the turn of the century, does not seem sufficient.

Secondly, he or she risks his or her own money in the process. I have drawn a firm line between functionaries – people drawing salaries, for example Heinrich Conreid, who ran the New York Metropolitan Opera for the Vanderbilts – and impresarios – for whom the alternative is making or losing a personal fortune.

Thirdly, the impresario does both these things persistently, on a grand scale, including the rich panoply of full orchestras, grand sets and popular stars. There were, of course, many smaller fish, excluded from my list by the modest or ephemeral nature of their enterprises: people like Lilian Baylis, who persevered with her aunt's creation (Sadler's Wells) on the frailest of shoestrings, thus laying the foundation of today's English National Opera; or Carl Rosa, who, though outstandingly successful in making money, tended to present distinctly second-class performances.

Impresarios rose and fell; a few made fortunes, like Rosa; others disappeared under multiplying debts, like E. T. Smith; some were habitually fraudulent, like Richard d'Oyly Carte; others spent their inherited fortunes in the pursuit of fame or music, like Sir Thomas Beecham. Although the type is extinct now, it was once a thriving species, and offers a rich choice of specimens to the biographer.

Three men elbowed their way into the foreground during my

researches, as being both more interesting in themselves, and more illustrative of the vanished world of individuals presenting grand opera: Mapleson, the epitome of music hall bragadoccio; Hammerstein, who worked all his life to make money to spend on opera; and Christie, who casually created a great and enduring institution by the exercise of firm leadership and as the result of a sublime indifference to obstacles. All three operated on the grandest scale, deploying resources now more usually associated with major corporations like Disney than with individual tycoons. The world they inhabited has passed away – their nearest equivalent today would be Robert Stigwood or Cameron Mackintosh, both of whom wisely shelter behind the corporate shield of limited liability.

I began my researches for this book with a number of preconceptions, some of which have subsequently been wholly contradicted by the facts. I was surprised by the overwhelming evidence that poor cash control, combined with the costs associated with *building* rather than with *making music*, lay at the heart of the ruin of those who failed. I discovered, again and again, that the colossal fees demanded by and paid to the reigning stars proved to be good business rather than bad, attracting a more than matching income from the public and from sponsors lured by the 'name'.

I

Opera
1597–1864

IN THE MIDDLE Ages, not much happened without the Church. Not much happened without the Church even as late as 1600. This, the year of the birth of the first Royal Command performance of an opera, was also the year of Giordano Bruno's death. He was burnt alive as a heretic for announcing that it was clear, from what he could see through his new telescope, that the earth was not the centre of a fixed, Aristotelian universe, as had previously been believed.

New ideas, then as now, are best approached with caution.

Throughout the sixteenth century, however, the grip of the Church on the arts was gradually being loosened. Monarchs diverted their architects' skills away from the building of cathedrals and towards raising palaces to their own glory; the Escorial, Chambord, the Louvre and Whitehall Palace began to glitter with a new and exuberant delight in art for art's sake.

Holbein started his career painting biblical scenes with perhaps just a glimpse of the devout donor cautiously peeping out of one corner, and moved on to labour on vast dynastic

5

family frescos for Henry VIII and his circle. Music was certain to be the next of the arts to be released into the secular domain.

At this time the city-state of Florence, grown rich from trading under the Medici dynasty, aesthetes as well as conquerors, was the crucible of progress in, and the rebirth of, the Arts. Just as the Florentine Renaissance architects delighted in discovering and making use of Classical sources and disciplines for their new buildings, so their clients began to debate how the Greeks might have fused music with drama for their entertainments. The feeling was that if they had not done so, then they should have.

In 1597 a group of these rich enthusiasts, calling themselves the *Camerata*, decided to put on an 'opera' in the private palazzo of their colleague Jacopo Corsi, a thirty-eight year old banker, silk merchant and amateur composer. The event would take place during the Florence Carnival.

This, the first opera we know about, was a work largely composed by the Medicis' Court Organist (and occasional tenor), Jacopo Peri, with at least one chorus contributed by Corsi himself. Entitled *La Dafne*, it is based on the legend of the river-god's daughter who, when pursued by the love-sick Apollo, is turned into a laurel tree by her over-protective mother. The score consists of arias, choruses and one piece of through-composed recitative, '*Qual' nova meraviglia*', the report of the nymph's frustrating metamorphosis.

So we see that in music, as in sculpture and painting, Greek mythology was considered the first socially acceptable alternative to purely religious subjects. The opera must have been a success with the invited audience: when Henri IV of France married Maria de' Medici three years later, opera was a part of the celebrations. At the Palazzo Pitti on 6 October 1600 was performed a second opera by Peri from an ancient Greek source – *L'Euridice*. Opera had definitely arrived.

Widespread success followed quickly. Opera's first big

'name', the Venetian Claudio Monteverdi (1567–1643), Court choirmaster first, until 1612, to the Gonzagas in Mantua, where he composed *Orfeo*, and thereafter to the Doges at San Marco, began to churn out a series of popular works. These led to the building, in 1637, of the first public opera-house, the Teatro Tron di San Cassiano in Venice; by 1799 *La Serenissima* boasted a total of nine small public theatres specialising in the presentation of opera. For example, the first performance of Monteverdi's *Combattimento di Tancredi e Clorinda* took place in the Palazzo Dandolo, now better known as the Hotel Danieli.

These beautiful but comparatively modest houses (the San Cassiano had six hundred seats, with an average attendance in 1659 of two hundred and seventy-two) could not compare with Duke Ranuccio Farnese's massive three and a half thousand-seater Gran Teatro dei Farnese. Completed in 1618 and built into the second floor of his palace at Parma, this had a proscenium arch, raked seating, and a stage measuring forty-one metres deep and twelve metres across. It also had cloud machinery, and a capacity actually to flood the auditorium to produce scenic islands: with this theatre the Duke set a standard that was to ruin many of his fellow enthusiasts over the next three centuries.

The progress of opera promotion in Italy was, therefore, from private enterprise on to public investment by way of Court patronage, a process which took all of forty years, and which soon came to be emulated throughout Continental Europe, where it has continued ever since.

In England, however, though its beginnings were similar, the development of opera followed a totally different path.

Shakespeare had used music in his plays (especially in *The Tempest*), and there was a growing tradition of extravagant Court masques which combined scenery, singing, dancing and poetry. An example was the private performance of a work by

Ben Jonson given at Althorp by Lord Spencer for King James I on his way south from Edinburgh in 1603 when he acceded to the throne of England.

These masques provided early employment for England's first Renaissance architect, Inigo Jones, and established what was to become a steady and enduring partnership, that between opera and architecture.

Just as architects worked on opera sets (Palladio, Jones and Vanbrugh), so opera-promoters down the ages have hugely turned to architectural expenditure (Lord Burlington, John Rich, Mapleson, Hammerstein and the Christie dynasty). Like music and maths, these two endeavours inter-connect, and not only out of practical necessity. There is an excitement, a massive grandeur inherent and achievable in both opera and architecture that tends to attract the same sort of personality.

On 23 May 1656 Sir William Davenant, holder since before the Civil War of the only Royal Patent to build a playhouse for drama and 'musical presentments' in London, produced his *First Dayes Entertainment at Rutland-House, by Declamations and Musick: after the manner of the Ancients*. Rutland House was his own home in Aldersgate Street, and he sold a hundred and fifty tickets:

> After a flourish of music, the curtains were drawn open, and the Prologue entered. First he apologised for the small dimensions of the room, the sideways disposition of the audience (in two groups facing each other), and the discomfort of the benches.

He then added:

> Think this your passage, and the narrow way
> To our Elysian field, the OPERA:
> Tow'rds which some way we have gone far about
> Because it seems so long since we set out.

8

The point is this: London's first night of opera – that is to say, sung music, rather than the general spectacle of a masque – was staged for profit, and it was staged without the benefit of any preliminary public expenditure. Nor does it seem to have occurred to seventeenth-century London, any more than to twentieth-century New York, that it should be done any other way. Indeed, *because* the promotion of opera in England was from the start seen as a business venture, it prospered accordingly. For example, in 1688 the barrister Christopher Rich paid eighty pounds (around twelve thousand pounds in 1998 terms) for a share in the Theatre Royal patent; he made so much money from this investment that he gave up his law practice to concentrate on presenting opera at Drury Lane, and also built a new theatre, the third on the Lincoln's Inn Fields site.

Christopher's son John Rich inherited this investment, and in 1728 proved himself as astute an impresario as his father by presenting John Gay's satirical smash hit, *The Beggar's Opera*. One hundred and five performances, in two consecutive seasons, brought John Rich a clear profit of more than seven thousand pounds.

Throughout this book, the question of comparison between the value of money then and now is important, in order to gauge the relative effect of the sums involved. The problem is that wage inflation has far outstripped increases in the cost of staple items such as milk, bread, et cetera, and this produces considerable distortion. However, since the overall rate of inflation between 1600 and 1939 was minuscule, although the graph climbs all but vertically thereafter, a simple calculation for 1998 is to multiply all figures by just over a hundred and fifty. This still underestimates the purchasing power of salaries, however. Before the introduction and expansion of income tax, when a singer could survive in comfort on forty-five pounds per annum and a nurse was considered well paid on a yearly twenty-four pounds, Rich's seven thousand was a princely profit indeed

– though not dissimilar to today's profits from presenting major, internationally successful musicals.

Such profits provide perhaps the clearest evidence that opera in the eighteenth and nineteenth centuries was the equivalent of pop music today, not only in its ethos, but also in the aura surrounding its most successful proponents. There was not the slightest suggestion of élitism: it was popular entertainment, and intended as such. That the concept does not belong entirely to history is exemplified by the 'Three Tenors', each earning a million pounds per performance.

His spectacular success with *The Beggar's Opera* led John Rich to emulate his father, even outdo him: he decided to build an even bigger theatre. He leased a piece of ground in Covent Garden, a hundred and twenty feet by a hundred, from Wriothesley, 3rd Duke of Bedford, for sixty-one years from Lady Day, 1731, at a rent of a hundred pounds per annum. His private quotation for the building work, from the architect James Shepherd, totalled just over five and a half thousand pounds.

The actor–manager Thomas Betterton had employed Sir John Vanbrugh to build a new theatre at the Haymarket in 1705, paid for by thirty investors subscribing a hundred pounds each, so Rich was already following established practice when he issued a prospectus, seeking to raise no less than fifteen thousand pounds, the sum which he claimed was needed to build and equip this enterprise.

Undismayed by a subscription of less than half this (but in itself an immediate profit for him of eleven hundred pounds), he went ahead with the new building. It was completed by November 1732, and opened with a play, Congreve's *Way of the World*. Rich charged five shillings in the pit, two shillings in the gallery, half that upstairs, and half a guinea (ten shillings and sixpence) for standing-room on the stage. This represented a maximum take of two hundred pounds per night, and Rich actually banked a hundred and fifteen pounds on the opening night.

The clearest proof that the presentation of both opera and

theatre was seen as just another business is that after the success of Betterton and Rich there was a rush to cash in, followed by the inevitable losses and failures.

Even composers joined the race to enrich themselves by investing in opera. As a salaried employee writing operas and teaching music, Handel had amassed savings of around ten thousand pounds. Having taught the Princess of Wales's children to play the harpsichord, he was also well placed to enlist Royal patronage, and he could even provide his own operas. How could he go wrong? Yet by 1736, eight years later, he was virtually bankrupt. For a start, opera singers were beginning to appreciate their own earning potential. Nicolo Nicolini, the great Neapolitan *alto castrato*, had negotiated a fee of eight hundred guineas for seven months' work at the Haymarket spread over three years, plus a hundred and fifty pounds for every new work he introduced. This established a bench-mark which every successful singer subsequently felt he had to beat, each trying to leap-frog over his peers to be 'the best' – or, rather, the most expensive.

Throughout the rest of the eighteenth and in the early nineteenth centuries, opera in Britain thrived in a widespread variety of minor endeavours.

Charles Dibdin, a versatile but prickly all-round entertainer and part-time composer, distinguished himself by trying to build *two* new theatres for his comic operas. The first, at the south end of Blackfriars Bridge and called the Royal Circus, was intended to double as a site for both tournaments and great operatic ventures – the Wembley Stadium of its day. By 1781 the Royal Circus was actually completed, but Dibdin's business venture as a whole failed and he spent 1784 in the King's Bench Prison, writing an account of what had happened. But the second theatre, at St Pancras, scarcely got off the ground – the preliminary superstructure was blown down in a storm.

Not that the audiences were any more perfect. When John Beard (1717–1791, married to Rich's daughter and known as the 'Greatest of British Tenors') inherited the lease of Covent Garden and took on its management in partnership with Thomas Arne, he presented Arne's expensive extravaganza *Artaxerxes*. Any illusions that eighteenth-century opera audiences were élitist, composed exclusively of the Georgian equivalent of the Institute of Directors, will be dispelled by knowing what occurred the night Beard announced that 'full prices' would be charged – that is to say, he withdrew the usual concessions. *The Gentleman's Magazine* reports that, rising as one, the crowd fell upon the opera house, 'all the benches of the boxes and pit being entirely torn up, the glasses and chandeliers broken, and the linings of the boxes cut to pieces.'

The speculative promotion of British opera was by no means confined to London. Just as the growing trade of the Empire brought increasing wealth to the capital, so also it disseminated the tastes of those at the centre. As early as 1733 an opera company is recorded as visiting Jamaica, but with mixed results:

They receiv'd 370 pistoles the first Night, to the *Beggar's Opera*; but within the Space of two Months they bury'd their third *Polly*, and two of their men. The Gentlemen of the Island, for some Time, took their Turns upon the Stage, to keep up the diversion; but this did not hold long; for, in two Months more, there were but one old Man, a Boy, and a Woman of the Company left: The rest died, either with the Country-Distemper, or the common Beverage, the noble Spirit of Rum-punch, which is generally fatal of Newcomers. The shatter'd Remains, with upwards of 2000 Pistoles in Bank, embark'd for Carolina, to join another Company at Charlestown, but were cast away in the voyage ...

In North America, a 'London Company of Comedians', led

first by Lewis Hallam and later by his widow, toured the cities on the eastern seaboard until the threat of war with England sent them to seek (comparative) safety in Jamaica.

Opera had become ultra-fashionable. Particular favourites were Gluck's *Orfeo* (sometimes with bits by Johann Christian Bach added as enrichments) and Arne's *Thomas and Sally*, and anything by Handel. The plan of the King's Theatre boxes in 1791 (at that time owned by the playwright Richard Brinsley Sheridan, over-borrowed as usual) shows ninety-one out of the hundred taken. The Prince of Wales, two other Royal dukes and the duchesses of Bedford, Marlborough, Ancaster, Buccleuch, Argyll and Richmond were among the subscribers, and boxes changed hands for as much as two and a half thousand pounds.

When sixteen people were trampled to death at the King's Theatre as it filled for a Royal Command performance of Storace's *No Song, No Supper*, the news was kept from George III and Queen Caroline in the Royal Box until after the play, to avoid disrupting the show. In 1807, at the age of twenty-seven, the theatre's principal diva, Angelica Catalani, was on the colossal salary of five thousand pounds for the season, while the theatre itself was only valued at forty thousand.

The nineteenth century brought a series of revolutions to opera, as it did to politics. The Romantic movement in literature created by Rousseau and Goethe was widely and successfully adapted into popular music, just as the new technologies enabled the building of bigger and better opera houses. Moreover, the profits from the Industrial Revolution, and from the long period of stability in Europe following the Treaty of Vienna, created an expanding middle class both eager and financially able to join in this fashionable means of entertainment.

In a sense, this widespread success sowed the seed of opera's future near-extinction, in that as the theatres were rebuilt bigger and yet bigger to accommodate the growing audiences – a rebuilding paid for by the profits accruing from these audiences – so the chorus grew to fill the larger stage, the orchestra grew to fill the larger pit, and those few singers who were able to compete against such forces grew the financial muscle to demand more pay. What had initially been a form of entertainment involving the employment of perhaps forty professionals was turning into one requiring four hundred or more, and thus inevitably becoming expensive when judged against the cost of the concerts or other entertainments of the day.

Opera, however, was *in*, and it was approaching its Golden Age, with a stream of popular works being produced by Bellini, Donizetti, Berlioz, Meyerbeer, and above all, Verdi.

The Golden Age of the Great Impresario can be roughly charted as between 1854 and 1914, since it was during those sixty years that all four main ingredients necessary for such an individual to flourish were most readily available: plenty of popular new works, a regular supply of magnificent new divas, a rich and growing clientele, and the technology and individual banking resources needed for building opera houses and presenting opera.

All opera houses were then still in private ownership. The impresario might build or buy a theatre himself, as did Hammerstein and Christie; but more probably he would lease it, like Smith, Gye, and Rosa, whether for a season of a few weeks, as Beecham did in 1911, or for a number of seasons, like Gye.

The impresario's outgoings would therefore be: rent; the purchase or rental of props, costumes and scenery; insurance against fire and theft; the salaries of the singers, orchestral players and general management and stage management staff; the promotional costs of advertising and promoting his presentations; and the cost of servicing and/or repaying any overdrafts or loans arising from a negative cash-flow. At his zenith Hammerstein was paying out over a million dollars a year, around thirty million pounds in 1998 terms. The turnover of Andrew Lloyd Webber's Really Useful Company in 1996 was £109 million.

Against this, the impresario had three main sources of income: subscriptions from enthusiastic backers, ticket sales through booksellers and others on commission, including the traditional tout, and ticket sales on the night. If these combined to a greater total than his expenses, he made a profit, which in the nineteenth century was largely tax-free; if not, he made a loss, and was liable to be imprisoned if he was unable to pay his debts. Like so many other failing businessmen, then as now, the impresario might, and often did, throw his own savings, his home and his other interests into the pot to try to stave off failure. In short, it was business, as usual, no more and no less.

As in most business enterprises, those who put on opera to make money got richer, like Carl Rosa and Richard d'Oyly Carte, and those who spent money in order to put on opera got poorer, like E. T. Smith and Sir Thomas Beecham.

But by 1911, the bubble was ready to burst. Richard Strauss's *Der Rosenkavalier*, scored for an orchestra of a hundred and eleven, provided surely the most poignant swan-song ever written, unconsciously tolling the knell of the Golden Age.

Opera had become so expensive in terms of the number of people necessary to stage and perform it that anything short of a sell-out success threatened any commercial producer with ruin. The Covent Garden seasons were being presented by an increasingly shaky syndicate, and Thomas Beecham's tremendous efforts there were made for the sake of the music, rather than for profit.

The Great War of 1914 to 1918 broke up the continuity of attendance, as well as cutting swathes through the customary audience, while the subsequent advent of the modernist composers known as the 'tuneless wonders' completed a cycle of decline which, if only very slowly, the combined propaganda of television and super-tenors is now beginning to reverse.

2

Colonel James Mapleson
(1830–1901)

HAVING BEEN REPEATEDLY urged by numerous friends on both sides of the Atlantic to set forth a few of the difficulties attending the career of an impresario who, during the last 30 years, has fought many operatic battles … I willingly sat down to the work, trusting that an account of the few partial defeats and the many brilliant victories incident to my life may be found interesting.

Thus, dated 21 September 1888 and written as from the fashionable Junior Carlton Club, open the *Memoirs* of 'Colonel' James Henry Mapleson, erstwhile violinist, tenor, agent, opera manager, impresario and general all-round mountebank, and their tone accurately speaks for the man.

Mapleson was born in London on 4 May 1830, and the late Harold Rosenthal, editor of the *Memoirs*, discovered the unexpected fact that his performing career began early, at just seventeen days old, when he was 'christened' on stage during a performance of *Henry VIII* at the Drury Lane Theatre.

Aged fourteen Mapleson entered the Royal Academy of Music under Cipriani Potter; it was then the only musical school in London, and catered for seventy students. Potter describes him as showing 'some disposition for the violin and pianoforte'. Mapleson recalled composing two piano pieces and a song, and by the age of eighteen he was playing first violin in the orchestra of the Royal Italian Opera, then based at Her Majesty's Theatre. His ambition, however, was already to leave the relative obscurity of the pit for the greater glamour of the stage, and the combined talents of Balfe (the composer of *The Bohemian Girl*), a leading tenor and a baritone were pressed into converting him into a singer, opening up what they all told him would be a fine career as a *primo tenore*.

At this point, an important *caveat* has to be introduced: a major source of the details of Mapleson's career is, of course, his own *Memoirs*. Even at the time of their publication they were viewed with some scepticism, and Rosenthal's meticulous research has certainly revealed a sturdy disregard for detail on Mapleson's part when the truth is less than flattering.

So it may be that Mapleson did have vocal talent. Or it may be that his tutors flattered their pupil. Or maybe he just heard from them what he wanted to hear. Certainly he crossed to Italy, and studied for three years under Professor Mazzucato of Milan. He first sang at Lodi, and then records that he was paid four pounds a month to sing at Verona, where he took over as Manrico in two performances of *Il Trovatore*.

Mapleson reports that he sang under the name of Enrico Mariani, but the most diligent research by Rosenthal has failed to uncover any record of these performances. In his *Memoirs*, on the other hand, Mapleson is conspicuously silent on the subject of the one appearance that *was* recorded, at Drury Lane, where his Alphonso in Auber's *Masaniello* attracted the attention of the *Morning Post*:

> The cast was excellent, with the exception of Mr Mapleson, a young gentleman who undertook, with considerable imprudence, the part of Alphonso. We have rarely met with

a person so thoroughly inexperienced in the ways of the stage, venturing a character of importance. The audience resented the attempt with but small mercy, and the unfortunate debutant was exposed to a fire of irony and laughter ... [23 July 1854]

He sang again, in a concert, but records that his throat became affected; this necessitated the surgical attentions of a Dr Billing, who removed both his uvula and his tonsils in one go.

Thus variously discouraged from pursuing his career as a tenor, two years later Mapleson set himself up in the Haymarket as a musical agent, supplying singers to Benjamin Lumley and Frederick Gye, the two main impresarios then presenting opera in London. He claims to have prospered greatly for two years, but when in 1858 E. T. Smith, the lessee of the Theatre Royal, Drury Lane, offered him the job of managing his opera season, Mapleson grabbed it, 'influenced by my love of the divine art'. Indeed, he was unusually well qualified for the task, having played both in the pit and on stage, in addition to his two years' experience of negotiating contracts as an agent.

The next year saw Mapleson's first (though far from last) appearance in court, where he was attempting to defeat an injunction brought by Frederick Gye (a rival impresario who held the lease of the Opera House at Covent Garden from its owner, the Duke of Bedford) to prevent Francesco Graziani, a baritone under contract to Gye, from appearing for Smith. The case lasted for two days; Sir Hugh Cairns led a large team for Smith, who lost.

Mapleson's memories of this period are richly flavoured. He describes how his time was divided between making peace on stage between rival bands of Italian musicians armed to the teeth and ready to kill for their jobs, and personally negotiating the marriage contract of the would-be Duchessa di Cirella (Smith's new Leonora, Mlle Carolina Guarducci) to ensure that the Duke actually married her (he did).

During 1860, at a time when Smith was becoming increasingly distracted by a variety of other ventures, including several restaurants and a milliner's shop bought on impulse in Brighton, it was Mapleson who travelled down to the operatically baroque Witley Court to negotiate a new lease for Smith from the landlord of Her Majesty's Theatre, Lord Dudley. Dudley had finally been driven to foreclose on Lumley, the previous lessee, over what the disgruntled Lumley described in his *Reminiscences* as the 'trifling question of three quarters' rent, scarcely exceeding £4,000' (in 1998 terms, about six hundred thousand pounds).

Smith was an exacting employer, given to announcing last-minute additions to the programme to please a sponsor, as for example when, for the Metropolitan Board of Works, he added a rendition of *The Waterman*, complete with a new song especially dedicated to the Board, on a night when Pauline Viardot was singing Donna Anna in *Don Giovanni*. He was also fond of arranging spontaneous celebrity appearances, such as that of two bruised prize-fighters fresh from their duel, who were put triumphantly on show in a private box until, exhausted, they were allowed to stagger home after the first act.

Smith's finest gimmick was his proposal for a double performance of *Trovatore*, to take place on a divided stage, one cast directly above the other, with Grisi singing Leonora on the lower floor in vertical competition with Therese Tietjens poised immediately above her head. The singers rebelled, and Mapleson in his *Memoirs* claims the credit for dissuading Smith from this unconventional scheme.

In the event, the season of 1860 was to be Smith's last. Now based at Her Majesty's Theatre (as the former King's Theatre had been renamed in 1837), his operations were punctuated by the regular appearance of bailiffs placing the company's costumes under distraint. Famous for his inability to distinguish between '*La Traviatore*' and '*Il Troviata*', Smith had for some time survived by hiring, for a pound a day, a one-thousand-pound

Bank of England note: startled suppliers would offer him temporary credit when they found themselves unable to give him change.

Unaware of his employer's true circumstances, Mapleson was already planning Smith's 1861 season, and had contracted an unknown nineteen year old soprano from America to sing four nights a week for forty pounds a week. Then Smith's bubble finally burst. Increasingly elusive, he eventually revealed that he had accepted four thousand pounds from Frederick Gye, his principal rival, to refrain from competing against him. This was a traditional business ploy, and one especially prevalent among impresarios; Smith took the money, paid his debts, and retired.

In his *Memoirs* Mapleson says it was the young American soprano, a Miss Adelina Patti of New York, who suggested that he should take Smith's place. She expressed confidence in her ability to attract an audience for him, but the arrangement proved more difficult to realise than it might seem, since Smith still held the lease of the theatre. Although he appeared to be delighted by the younger man's initiative, Mapleson found, when the contract for a sub-lease was finally produced, that the small print contained a notable restriction: 'Italian Opera excepted'.

Her Majesty's Theatre was the leading house associated with opera at this time, able to seat more than three thousand. Covent Garden, seating only two thousand, intermittently came a respectable second, depending on its various lessees. But Covent Garden was currently monopolised by Gye and his supporters, and so the only other theatre suitable for Mapleson's venture was the Lyceum; this he managed to secure. He then travelled to Marseilles, where Lumley, the previous lessee of Her Majesty's, was recovering. Lumley was a solicitor who had been lured into the world of opera, disastrously, as things turned out, by his employment first as lawyer to Pierre François Laporte, manager of London's Italian Opera, and then as co-executor in winding up the estate after Laporte's bankruptcy and death. Mapleson bartered the contracts of singers already signed up by Lumley in return for half his potential gross nightly receipts, but got back to London only to find that Patti had signed on with Gye instead.

Undeterred, he opened on 8 June 1861 with Therese Tietjens singing Leonora in *Il Trovatore*. The following night she sang the lead in *Lucrezia Borgia*, and at the same time, she and the company were rehearsing Verdi's new opera, *Un Ballo in Maschera*, after dinner, in order to get it ready to put on just six days before Gye's rival production at Covent Garden. This punishing regime was not unusual, though it may seem so today. Sir Charles Santley, the leading English baritone of the time, recorded being expected to sing a hundred and ten times in a five-month season, in conjunction with continuous rehearsing.

This performance of *Un Ballo in Maschera*, a great success with critics and public, settled Mapleson into what was to be his life's career. This time, he was evidently determined to make a success of it. He had his casts, including the doughty Miss Tietjens, a Hungarian of massive range and equally redoubtable carriage, up rehearsing all night, and he rearranged the stalls' seating so as to squeeze in another two rows. When the (English) chorus went on strike in mid-performance of Act 4 of Meyerbeer's *Les Huguenots*, he instructed the principals to proceed without them. The chorus immediately gave in, but he sacked them all, saying that he would not only never give any of them a job again, but that thereafter he would import his choruses from Italy.

Luigi Arditi, his conductor, wrote later:

Mapleson proved, during his short and venturesome season at the Lyceum, that he was a man of great energy and indefatigable perseverance. Many important works were thoroughly prepared, well sustained and competently managed …,

adding, 'Mapleson was, unlike Smith, a musician.'

Physically, Mapleson was a tall man, with broad shoulders, a wide forehead, and a pugnacious nose. He wore the conventional moustache and heavy mutton-chop whiskers of that era, and one of his American sopranos records that he was 'of gentlemanly appearance, always polite and with winning manners – a perfect English type.' An interviewer speaks of a strong, mellow voice.

There was something else – a natural penchant for showmanship, accompanied by the professional showman's traditional lack of principles. He had joined the Volunteers in 1858, and qualified as a sergeant, which entitled him to half a guinea a time for drilling recruits. Billeted at Walton-on-the-Naze in Essex, he found that just drilling his soldiers was not enough to attract the interest of the local girls. The twenty-eight year old Mapleson therefore had posters printed, advertising that Blondin, the famous tightrope-walker, would walk on his tightrope from Walton pier to the hotel where Mapleson was billeted. A huge crowd appeared, Mapleson marched up and down drilling his recruits, the Regimental Band played ... and a telegram was delivered which announced Blondin's unavoidable absence through illness. And there you have Mapleson – successful in producing the girls, but his success based upon a flimsy deception. It was a dangerous lesson for him to learn, and did nothing to deter him.

Mapleson himself reports that his first season at the Lyceum lost eighteen hundred pounds, but he plunged straight back in: he obtained four thousand pounds in advance subscription sales, and handed this over to Lord Dudley in return for a twenty-one year lease of Her Majesty's Theatre.

A typical Maplesonian confusion immediately arose. Mapleson believed this money represented security against rent to be paid in the future, while Lord Dudley asserted that it was part of the first year's rent, paid in advance, and that a further four thousand was required as a deposit before Mapleson could enter into the lease. It seems that Mapleson was a man who, while he perfectly understood opera-making, was not always wise in the basic essentials of commercial undertakings, high among which ranks the need to read a contract carefully before signing it.

Nevertheless, he raised the extra money from friends and supporters, and entered his new theatre with, he says, just two pounds to his name. He managed to cram in another three rows of stalls, but was subjected to the machinations of Gye who sent an emissary to Miss Tietjens with a blank contract, inviting her to fill in her own fee to move to Covent Garden. To this the prima donna rather unexpectedly replied, 'I have given my word to Mr Mapleson, which is better than all contracts.'

Mapleson's second season in London passed off profitably, but as soon as he left to tour the provinces with Verdi's *Trovatore* and Donizetti's *Lucrezia Borgia*, the drawbacks of management-on-a-shoestring became apparent. Having saved the cost (and heartache) of employing understudies, he lost his main contralto, who went down with influenza. The company got through a performance of *Lucrezia Borgia* with no Maffio Orsini well enough, but the next night produced an Azucena (the old gypsy in *Trovatore*) who sat silently on a sofa while her colleagues gallantly essayed ensembles with one line notably absent.

The third day, with no improvement in the afflicted throat, Mapleson decided to present an opera which did not require a principal contralto. He chose Bellini's *Norma*, in which the role of Adalgisa, contrary to modern practice, was then usually sung by a soprano.

The first scene was a success, but when the orchestra played the entrance of Pollione (the principal tenor), nothing happened. After a frantic gesture from Mapleson, the conductor played the introduction again ... again nothing stirred. The curtain was lowered 'amidst deafening protests from the audience'. Rushing backstage, Mapleson found that a struggle had broken out between his two main tenors as to which of them should go on; one, Antonio Giuglini, would, if he performed, be due by contract an extra hundred and sixty pounds.

Back in London, the same Giuglini in his turn succumbed to influenza, leaving Mapleson with six hundred pounds-worth of tickets sold and no one to sing that night in Flotow's *Martha*. In his *Memoirs* he recounts with relish how, as he was returning home in despair, his hansom cab all but ran over a man in the street who 'turned out to be a tenor'. Despite Therese Tietjens' protests, Mapleson insisted the man should go on, offering the probably very sound advice that, whenever he was in doubt, he should just keep on singing '*M'appari*', the main hit number of the show.

Thus the hallmark of Mapleson's career was settled early on: a good show if he could manage it, but a show there must be – anything to avoid refunding the takings to the ticket-holders.

Mapleson's third season, in 1863, included the British première of Gounod's *Faust*. He talked Chappell the music publishers into sponsoring the event to the tune of two hundred pounds, with the promise of another two hundred if he put on more than four performances; he then crossed the Channel and for a hundred pounds persuaded Charles François Gounod himself to come to London to supervise the production.

Mapleson usually acted as producer of his company's productions – in so far as that modern term had any meaning, since the 'concept production' of the late twentieth century was unknown in the nineteenth century. Santley records that when one company lost its experienced stage manager, chaos resulted as each singer went his or her own way.

On this occasion Mapleson also doubled as his own ticket agent. So slow were the sales through the box-office that he instructed his staff to say that the first three performances were sold out; he then hawked the tickets round the local shops (offering further free tickets as commission), and thus achieved both respectable houses for the start, and crowded ones for the later shows.

Yet again, Mapleson's control of his artists proved uncertain: an immense hullabaloo arose backstage when he booked the lead tenor for the wrong night. Only by dashing from one house to another, here cancelling the tenor's evening arrangements (while the poor man was still on the train south from Crewe, quite unaware of what was happening), and there dragging an ailing colleague from his bed and dosing him with a pint of claret mixed with raw eggs and sugar, was he able to assemble a cast.

Even then the police had to be engaged to prevent his Marguerite from walking out, and he had to calm down two hysterical sopranos. After all this effort, what the public actually saw was the tenor originally booked to sing Faust, hurriedly shaved of his moustache and singing his own wife's contralto role of Siebel, with whose music he was as uncertain as his replacement was with Faust's.

Charles Santley, who joined the company in Dublin to sing Valentine, records that on one occasion a muddle between Mapleson and his stage manager resulted in Mephistopheles being plunged through his trap-door, just as he'd opened his mouth to sing. Worse still, when they returned to London, he himself was made by Mapleson to swap roles and sing Mephistopheles, opposite an equally confused Faust sung by Swift:

> As usual he [Swift] did not know his music, and was quite innocent of the stage business. Whenever I had to address him, I could not find him; throughout the opera, whenever we had a few bars' rest, he left the scene to take care of itself, and retired to the wings to study what was coming.

November 1864 found Mapleson in Paris, looking for talent, and hearing the great soprano Christine Nilsson for the first time, in *The Magic Flute* at the Théâtre Lyrique. But nothing he saw changed his management style. When Santley rejoined him in Dublin (then an invariable part of any round-Britain tour) he was persuaded, this time by Therese Tietjens herself, to take on the role of the Duke of Ferrara, at about two hours' notice. He recounts how she pleaded with him: 'If you don't sing, the theatre must be closed. You hear that poor man hardly knows a note of his part and Swift is so hoarse he can scarcely make a sound.' It is an indication of how far the singers themselves could and did become infected with their employer's standards that Santley should have noted later: 'The curtain dropped to a storm of howling and hissing; but we had saved the performance and went home content.'

Santley himself was a model of phlegmatic calm in what must have been a maelstrom of nerves and discord. When part of Mapleson's stage set caught fire in the last act of *The Magic Flute*, and Santley's own children were at risk of being crushed as the audience stampeded for the exits, it was he (as Papageno) who strode to the front of the stage, grasping a panic-stricken Papagena, and bellowed 'Don't act like fools! It's nothing!'

Nor should Mapleson be condemned as more unscrupulous than his contemporaries. When Santley visited Newark, New Jersey with Carl Rosa's company, he was to sing the (transposed) title role in Ferdinand Hérold's very popular success *Zampa*. Just before the curtain went up, Santley was approached by the genial Rosa who asked if he'd mind just announcing that they were going to have to change the opera (to a *mélange*) because the orchestral parts for *Zampa* had been left behind. Such accidents did happen, so Santley strolled onto the stage and announced the change.

North American audiences were as noted then as they are now for their concentration on the music and their politeness to the artists: one can therefore imagine Santley's astonishment when the audience roared with fury, erupted from their seats and stormed the stage, tearing up their programmes and throwing the pieces at him. Indeed the entire performance (in which he sang parts from various operas, though always dressed as

27

Zampa) was continually interrupted by growls of angry dis-
approval. Only afterwards did Rosa reluctantly admit that precisely the same thing had happened when he sold tickets for
Zampa in Newark the year before.

In 1866 Mapleson was employing the famous soprano Giulia
Grisi ('a sad sight', Santley records ungallantly), fading now after
her heyday during the 1840s, when Frederick, Lord Castlereagh
and her husband had fought a duel over her favours (she had
given birth to an illegitimate child of the former). The daughter
of a Napoleonic general, the first Norina, and a great favourite
of Queen Victoria, she had married a French *marquis* before
setting up with 'Mario', the great Italian tenor born the
Cavaliere di Candia, whom she met on the stage of Her
Majesty's when they were both singing in *Lucrezia Borgia*, he
Gennaro, she Lucrezia. For the next twenty-two years they were
inseparable, whether at his Villa Salviati near Florence, their
château in France, or their London house. London and Paris were
then the two most lucrative markets for top sopranos, and Grisi
divided her time between them. They were, for years, the golden
couple of grand opera, the Alagna and Gheorghiu of their time.

The deal was that Grisi would work free for Mapleson so long
as he employed her husband Mario at three hundred pounds a
week (forty-five thousand, at 1998 prices: the other main principals were paid twenty-five guineas a show, the equivalent of
between three and a half and four thousand pounds today, and
a reasonable and comparable fee). Yet still Mapleson was
making money. No wonder he felt able to dine at home during
performances, although on one occasion he was summoned to
the theatre by a servant in a cab when the last act was held up
because the tenor singing the Duke of Mantua in that night's
Rigoletto had lost his temper over his costume and was threat-
ening everyone in sight.

The next year Mapleson added Christine Nilsson, an unusually beautiful young Swedish soprano noted for her pure if
undisciplined voice, to his cast. The company – Nilsson, the

faithful Tietjens, Santley, Mario and Zelia Trebelli – gave the British première of Verdi's *La Forza del Destino* at the same time as Mapleson's rival Gye was presenting the première of *Don Carlos* at Covent Garden.

That autumn Mapleson took the unusual step of engaging a female percussionist for his orchestra, an event which provoked immediate threats of an all-out strike by the increasingly muscular Musicians' Union, supported by their fellow trades unions. Mapleson, always combative, countered with individual writs against each of his musicians, but this particular confrontation failed to materialise. He had sub-let Her Majesty's Theatre for some Japanese performances and was dining with Tietjens at her house in St John's Wood on the night of 6 December, when the party was disturbed by an inarticulate servant who could only point distractedly out of the window at a great red glow in the distance. 'That's not the dawn ... that's the *theatre!*'

When he got there, Mapleson found soldiers in charge, and although he was allowed up to his office to salvage what papers he could, he was in such a state that when he reappeared he was only carrying a dress coat and his opera hat. *The Times* reports that the theatre 'burnt itself out and crumbled away in a towering pyramid of flame.' Tietjens herself lost twelve hundred pounds-worth of jewellery.

Mapleson did at least have the presence of mind to get Henry Jarrett, his business manager, out of bed and send him round to the Clapham home of F. B. Chatterton, the lessee of the Drury Lane Theatre, in order to book that theatre for March to July, before Chatterton should hear of the disaster. When Jarrett reached Clapham, a copy of *The Times* with the news of the fire on page 9 was actually lying on Chatterton's hall table. Jarrett placed his coat over it, and by 9.30 was able to leave with the signed lease of the Drury Lane Theatre in his pocket.

Just one hour later, Gye himself arrived in his carriage to offer Chatterton two hundred pounds a week provided he did *not* let the theatre to Mapleson. Such were the vicissitudes of life before the age of the telephone.

Mapleson, whose twelve thousand pounds-worth of scenery and effects were, predictably, uninsured (while Lord Dudley had the building and its library covered for seventy thousand), received a telegram of sympathy from Queen Victoria, and had the pleasure of conducting the Prince of Wales through the ruins before retiring to bed for a fortnight.

Refreshed by this interlude, he then went back on the road, this time to Glasgow; he records that all his *prime donne* cheerfully acted as seamstresses in making new costumes to replace those destroyed.

As if their recurrent rivalry and the constant threat of fire and bankruptcy were not enough, Gye and Mapleson were now jointly approached by a shadowy philanthropist named Wagstaff. To Mapleson he offered twenty thousand pounds in cash for any remaining operatic effects and the goodwill of his business, and three thousand a year to manage the Italian Opera at Covent Garden. His terms for buying out Gye's interest at Covent Garden were so generous that Gye went straight out and bought twenty thousand acres in Scotland, and at the same time began negotiations to sell his London house and buy a further large estate in Oxfordshire.

Mapleson saw through all this, and in his *Memoirs* claims the credit for warning Gye just in time that they were the victims of a lunatic. There was, surprisingly, one substantial benefit to arise out of this shared experience. At the end of the spring season, Mapleson received a letter:

Springfield House,
Wandsworth Road,
June 19th 1868

Dear Mr Mapleson,
The last time you were over here I believe we were pretty well agreed that our interests lay rather in the combination of the

two operas than in fighting one another. As we shall both of us be making our engagements for the next year, if anything is to be arranged between us it is time it were thought about. I should be very glad to see you on the subject … It would perhaps be well if we did not meet either at Drury Lane or at Covent Garden. Would you mind coming over here, or would you prefer our meeting somewhere in town? This matter, for obvious reasons, had better remain strictly *between ourselves* for the present.

It was signed by Frederick Gye.

The two men met, inevitably disagreed on terms, but finally thrashed out a contract whereby they became partners on a fifty-fifty basis for three years, with the arrangement to be kept secret for six months. Gye engineered the resignation of Sir Michael Costa, his musical director, of whose perfectionist dictatorship he had tired; Mapleson did not renew his lease on Drury Lane, but instead rented Covent Garden that autumn (Gye's own lease being only for the summer season). There were two reasons for this manoeuvre: the first, ostensible reason was to enable Mapleson to continue to present opera, but the second, private one was so that he and Gye could meet without arousing suspicion of their collaboration.

The subterfuge worked. Even the clear-sighted Santley believed that it all happened just by chance, as a consequence of Lord Dudley making difficulties over extending Mapleson's lease to cover the new theatre to be built at Her Majesty's.

The accounts of Mapleson's and Gye's great 'Coalition' season of 1869 make cheerful reading:

Income:		
	Private subscriptions	£12,000
	Agents' subscriptions	£29,000
	Fees for concerts, etc.	£10,000
	Box office sales	£29,000
	Total:	£80,000

Expenditure:	Artists' salaries	£22,000
	Chorus & expenses	£13,000
	Orchestra	£ 7,500
	Sundries	£ 2,000
	Total:	£44,000

PROFIT · £36,000

Out of Mapleson's half-share, he paid three thousand pounds for insurance and the Poor Rates, as Gye was providing the theatre. An income of fifteen thousand pounds a year was riches indeed: even Jane Austen's Mr Darcy, with half Derbyshire, had only ten thousand. Mapleson, understandably, felt his hour had arrived.

But the coalition between Gye and Mapleson had left a vacuum in the opera world, and news of their huge profits made new competition inevitable. The hapless Lumley had now returned to his law practice, and to writing. Lest anyone should be tempted to believe that the world of opera has changed over the last hundred and fifty years, Lumley lamented in 1864 'the fact of there being no new first-rate composer in Europe' (thus dismissing Verdi, Berlioz, Bizet, Gounod, Wagner and Meyerbeer, all of whom were then producing new work). He also complained of the British government's unique meanness in refusing to grant the munificent subsidies readily available elsewhere throughout mainland Europe: 'Nowhere', he wrote, 'has the manager to struggle with such fearful hazards as in *England.*'

With Laporte dead, Smith bankrupt and Lumley demoralised, it was hardly surprising that the threat, when it materialised, should have come from one of Mapleson's own associates, one of those who were best able to judge his strengths and vulnerabilities.

Henry Jarrett, Mapleson's business manager, who had himself been briefly (and disastrously) involved in running an opera company with the musical publisher George Wood, turned agent and signed up Nilsson, Trebelli and several other singers, who thereby became available only through him; meanwhile, his erstwhile partner Wood leased the Theatre Royal in Drury Lane.

Gye, determined not to lose the new-found peace and prosperity of promoting opera without competition, suggested that the equal partnership with Mapleson be changed to bring Wood into the equation, on the basis of a half-share to Gye and a quarter-share each to Mapleson and Wood. After spirited discussion, he reluctantly conceded the principle of equal one-third shares. The three conspirators were poised to sign when Jarrett burst dramatically in upon them and demanded a word with Wood, as a result of which the deal foundered.

Baulked in this plan, Gye tried a different tactic. He negotiated a lease of the new Her Majesty's Theatre now rising from the ashes of its predecessor, which was to be held jointly in his name and Mapleson's. This lease, which had to be signed by 1 September, was for up to twenty-one years, even though the personal contract between Mapleson and Gye had only another two years to run.

What, asked Mapleson not unreasonably, would happen if he and Gye fell out? Gye would still have Covent Garden, but Mapleson would be paying half the rent on the new theatre and might be blocked by his partner from presenting opera there. He added a codicil to the effect that if his partnership with Gye should founder, the lease of Her Majesty's would revert to him alone.

Gye refused to sign, the time limit passed, and the contract failed. Gye then agreed with Lord Dudley a lease on Her Majesty's in his own name only; Mapleson tried to sue both Dudley and Gye, and cancelled his partnership with Gye; and Jarrett was busily hawking Nilsson's services about, ready to settle with the first person willing to pay her two hundred pounds per show. In short, everything had returned to normal.

Mapleson went back to Drury Lane, where Wood and Jarrett had gone under – again – and relates with ill-concealed glee that within a short time Lord Dudley was suing Gye for seven and a half thousand pounds in rent arrears.

For three seasons Mapleson remained happily at Drury Lane, shrugging off such incidental irritations as losing first his new tenor Italo Campanini, who was offered a five hundred per cent increase in salary to go to the United States, and then his new soprano, Emma Albani – to Gye, because she went to the wrong opera house when she arrived in London, and Gye got her to sign a contract before revealing her mistake. As well as working for him, she then married his elder son, Ernest Gye.

Even so, Mapleson was thriving. The Prince of Wales had taken a box at the Theatre Royal, and Mapleson now had the services of London's pre-eminent conductor, Sir Michael Costa, who was only too delighted to work against Gye. He was also able to flaunt the fashionable tenor Italo Campanini, at least until his defection to the United States, as well as his old favourites Tietjens, Trebelli, and Nilsson. Nilsson's fee from Mapleson of two hundred pounds a night caused endless trouble for Gye at Covent Garden: he had recruited Patti at eighty pounds a night, but subsequently had to agree to raise this to two hundred guineas. There were also new stars like Marie Roze, who in an echo of the Albani–Gye alliance married Mapleson's eldest son Henry.

On top of the London season, Mapleson was touring between sixty and seventy provincial towns during the summer, then moving north to Manchester, and culminating with fourteen weeks in Dublin at Christmas. Apart from the music hall, opera was the major form of public entertainment, and its salaries, and costs, were affected accordingly. Mapleson's apotheosis, in 1873, was the State Visit of the Shah of Persia. The Shah, having announced that he would attend the first half of a Mapleson performance (Act 1 of *Traviata*, followed after the interval by Act 1 of *Mignon*), arrived just in time for the interval, after which he was supposed to leave for another scheduled engagement at the Goldsmith's Hall.

The Prince of Wales told Mapleson to bring Nilsson to be presented to the Royal party before they left; but when he got to her dressing-room Mapleson found that Nilsson – who had just angrily sung '*Sempre libera*' to an empty Royal Box – had already changed from her Violetta ball-gown into her rags for Mignon, and showed not the least disposition to put herself out to meet the errant potentate. Mapleson begged, and begged; eventually she agreed, to save him further embarrassment. Following him into the ante-room of the Royal Box, she marched up to the Shah, who was eating peaches, and told him he was '*un très mauvais Shah*', brandishing her bare foot at him to show how poorly she was now dressed.

The great man was so impressed by this that he insisted on staying for the second half of the performance, thus abandoning the Master of the Goldsmiths, the Lord Mayor, the Sheriffs and all the other assembled civic dignitaries to a three-hour wait, standing in line. Mapleson was ecstatic.

His military career had also been prospering: by 1869 he had reached the rank of Lieutenant-Colonel in the 6th (Volunteer) Tower Hamlet Rifles, from which eminence he threw himself energetically into drilling every regiment he came into contact with on his opera tours. Soldiers from the Scots Fusiliers at Richmond and the Beggars' Bush Barracks at Dublin, the 5th Fusiliers at Glasgow's Gallowgate Barracks, the Scots Guards at Windsor, the 100th at Salford, even the Grenadier Guards at Wellington Barracks, wheeled and stamped under Mapleson's delighted eye. Asked how he was able to find the time for this unusual distraction, he wrote, from the heart:

> Frequently at the end of a long rehearsal I have, without finding time to dine, had to put on my uniform, get on horseback, and hurry to take command of my regiment in the Regent's or Hyde Park. The entire change of occupation was,

I am convinced, the best possible relaxation I could have. I never could have recruited my energies by simple idleness, which, besides being in my case intolerable, is apt to lead one into scrapes.

And the prompt unquestioning obedience of his troops must have been a most welcome relief from his experiences on- or back-stage.

The year 1875 saw the triumphant start of what was Mapleson's mightiest venture, and also his most crushing defeat. For some time he had been dreaming a great dream: a brand-new, purpose-built National Opera House, on the same scale as the Palais Garnier (only just completed, with 1,991 seats, it had been commandeered as a food store during the Commune) and the Vienna Hofoper (equally new, having just opened in 1869 with 2,200 seats), and with himself as its all-conquering *intendant*.

This was not so very wild a target. Not only had there been considerable pressure for just such a project, with discussions that eventually led to the founding of the Royal College of Music predicated on just such a building, but this was also the time when Victorian construction work was reaching its apogee. With the Crimean War safely over, London resonated with great building projects – the Victoria (Thames) Embankment, the new Museums, new Ministries in Westminster, above all the Foreign Office, newly completed for Queen Victoria's forty-ninth birthday on 24 May 1868. Indeed, whole tracts of farmland in Kensington and Bayswater were being smothered in brick-dust and cement. It was only five years since the Royal Academician Harry Newton had produced a serious scheme for rebuilding the Law Courts and some government offices in the middle of the Thames; why, then, should there not be a new opera house too?

And with opera still seen only as a strictly commercial undertaking (it is impossible to imagine Mr Gladstone proposing to raise taxes for the presentation of Italian opera), who better to lead it than Mapleson? At forty-five he was twenty years younger than Frederick Gye, his only real rival in London; otherwise, there was just a scattering of minor managers touring the provinces with their small-scale travelling troupes.

Smirke's rebuilding of the Covent Garden theatre in 1809 to seat an audience of 2,800 had cost almost a hundred and fifty thousand pounds. Mapleson's plan was to build an immense National Opera House, as large as any on the Continent, to maximise both spectacle and receipts: as with all Mapleson's endeavours, this one was based on maximum bombast and minimum concentration of actual cash-flow.

No doubt his negotiations over the site he chose, on the Victoria Embankment, were facilitated by his previous contacts with the Metropolitan Board of Works: they had been responsible for the construction of the Embankment, and the old foreshore badly needed new buildings to smarten it up.

The cost of the Embankment, in essence the shoring-up of the north bank of the Thames to enable the Metropolitan Railway to run alongside it, was largely met by Government grants. The site Mapleson wanted extended to almost two acres beside the river, and he proposed to share this with a relocated Royal Academy of Music, the Lyric Club, a picture gallery, and a sub-station of the Metropolitan (underground) Railway, especially built to bring his customers to him. There was even to be a subterranean passage to the Houses of Parliament, as well as Turkish baths, changing-rooms for audience as well as cast, a billiards room, a doctors' surgery, and a company river-steamer, commissioned from Thorneycrofts, as well as an immense houseboat for concerts and excursions on the Thames.

The design, over a framework of iron by Francis Fowler in *style Rothschild*, was described by *The Times* as 'an irregular parallelogram with a cupola rising to 150 feet'. Not surprisingly, questions were asked in the House of Commons about the ethics of allowing an entrepreneur to build on land reclaimed from the river at the rate-payers' expense. It should not be supposed, however, that this would have unduly dismayed those who had subscribed to the scheme under the usual inducements of 'owning' boxes and seats (an arrangement which survives to this day in the contemporary scheme at the Royal Albert Hall). In the City financial circles of this time, as faithfully portrayed in the novels of Anthony Trollope, to make money fast, at whoever's expense, was the principal aim, and in the heyday of Imperial preference there was no shortage of money seeking new places to grow. Moreover, everyone enjoyed his collection of ancient British swords which he displayed together with the tusks and skulls of prehistoric beasts – all alleged to have been dug from the foundations of a site which had only recently been artificially created by the embanking contractors.

A modest ceremony took place on 7 September 1875 when Miss Tietjens contrived to lay the first brick – assisted by the architect holding her arm, the engineer holding the trowel, and the foreman holding the said brick, and accompanied by cheering from the six hundred men happily employed on the project. This was followed by a less modest ceremony on a 'raw and gloomy' December morning when, under a marquee festooned with flags and bunting, to the sound of the combined military bands of the Coldstream Guards and the Honourable Artillery Company, and watched by a great crowd seated on benches covered with scarlet cloth, the young Duke of Edinburgh (Queen Victoria's second son, then aged thirty-one), supported by the Lord Mayor and all the usual worthies, took a 'richly chased trowel' from Mapleson's hands and laid the first stone.

Preparations for this event had led to Mapleson being invited in October to Eastwell Park, the great house rented by the Edinburghs in Kent. The visit got off to a wobbly start when he was met at Ashford station by two coaches, one for himself and the other for his luggage. As he had only brought with him a small bag holding a tail-suit and a stiff shirt, Mapleson suffered somewhat from the servants' incredulous smiles.

The evening's entertainment consisted of listening to the Edinburghs squabbling over their duets for piano and violin; but worse was to follow. The next morning he was taken off first by the Duchess (the twenty-one year old daughter of Czar Alexander II, and imperious with it) to admire her fish-pond, and then, having brought with him no outdoor clothes or boots, to accompany the Duke on a shooting expedition in the pouring rain. Around they traipsed, Mapleson wet through and his shoes so soaked that, when the leather dried indoors, they shrank, and he had real trouble getting them off.

Nor was his ordeal over. A second evening followed, this time with the Duke challenging him to billiards and then proceeding to lose. Try as Mapleson might, he could not help getting ahead. 'I saw from the expression of the Duchess's countenance, that she had set her heart upon her husband's defeating me', but to his mounting horror he found himself within two points of the game, and with the balls in such a position that it was almost impossible, with any degree of plausibility, to avoid hitting them both. He managed it; but the visit was obviously a great trial for him.

By the day of the December ceremony it was common knowledge that the foundations had cost Mapleson thirty-three thousand pounds, rather than the two and a half thousand he had budgeted for, because of the appalling conditions of the site. The contractors had had to dig fifty feet down to find any sturdy London clay for their footings, and all the while water poured into the excavations: fifteen or more steam-driven pumping engines were required to keep the work dry.

It was already a disaster, but Mapleson persevered. After the ceremony, when the Duke had gone, the rest settled down to a great celebratory lunch. After the toasts, Mapleson rose to speak:

Although I am the originator of this scheme, I could have done little but for the kind way I have been supported by all ranks, from the highest in the land downwards. Before taking any step in this enterprise, I have felt myself bound to be provided with sufficient resources for carrying it through, and I heartily acknowledge the ready response I have met with from all quarters.

This was cheered with enthusiasm, and there must have been many investors present who were greatly relieved to hear his words. But it was all puff. By the time the builders reached eaves-level, towards the end of 1877, the money Mapleson had raised, a massive hundred and three thousand pounds, was completely exhausted. A further ten thousand pounds was needed to roof the building, a necessary stage for drawing down the additional mortgage of fifty thousand pounds he had negotiated for the fitting-out of the interior. To his horror, and initial disbelief, the bankers refused to budge.

There was Mapleson, with a gargantuan hundred-foot-high shell, one hundred thousand pounds paid out (around fifteen million pounds today), and no one was prepared to help him pay for its roofing. 'For starting a new sporting club,' he complained, 'the money could have been found in a few hours.' In our own day, the Channel Tunnel and the new British Museum Library have both proved to be projects simply too big to be junked, but this was not the case with Mapleson's great dream. Those responsible for making the decision must have judged that neither his track record in administering the construction nor the likely receipts were such as to inspire confidence in a sensible return on any further capital injected into the scheme.

The pumping engines fell silent, the builders drifted away unpaid; Mapleson, so often in the past badgered by creditors, was now beset as never before by furious investors. Finally came the ultimate and public humiliation: the great shell was sold to speculators for twenty-nine thousand pounds. They failed in their turn, and re-sold the ruins, for five hundred pounds, to a purchaser who then had to pay a further three thousand to have the huge walls demolished.

In 1886 the site was acquired for the newly-formed Metropolitan Police. On its expensive foundations now stands Norman Shaw's 1887 Scotland Yard, built of Dartmoor granite and Portland stone quarried by convicts. 'The site of what ... would have been the finest theatre in the world, is now to serve for a new police-station,' noted Mapleson ruefully. But his irrepressible good nature breaks though, and he adds: 'With such solid foundations, the cells, if not comfortable, will at least be dry.'

The failure of this venture was the total ruination of all his hopes. In view of his reaction to the theatre fire, one might have expected him on this occasion to take to his bed for several months. Yet he did not; and that such a crushing calamity, entailing both public humiliation and substantial personal losses, in no way deflected him from his continuing efforts suggests that he had long anticipated the outcome, and had grown to accept it. The conductor Arditi, who knew him as well as anyone, wrote later:

> Mapleson was ... gifted with rare amenity and amiability of manner. He was seldom out of humour; he knew exactly how to manage his artists and, what is better, his creditors ... his manner was quite irresistible; there never lived a man whose suave, gentle art in calming the irrepressible creditor was more conspicuous or effective. To do him every justice, he paid his debts when he had money; but when the safe was empty he knew how to rid himself of tiresome and embarrassing duns with remarkable graciousness and admirable tact.

Even so, the collapse of the National Opera House project would have put a strain on anybody's command of graciousness and tact, so it is perhaps not surprising that Mapleson should

41

have chosen this moment to absent himself from London and turn his attention instead towards the prospects of opera promotion across the Atlantic.

During 1876, before Mapleson's hopes had been totally extinguished, he had continued his winter 'milk round' tour, of as many as sixty towns, as usual. When, in the following spring of 1877, the lessor of Drury Lane tried to cut himself into a profitable side-line Mapleson had developed in Shakespearian drama, the latter promptly moved back to Her Majesty's.

Lord Dudley had rebuilt the theatre but, understandably perhaps, was not keen to lease it to Mapleson again; instead, he offered the lease for sale, at thirty thousand pounds. Mapleson got back in by the subterfuge of offering six thousand on deposit against a possible sale (thus, incidentally, saving himself a thousand pounds against the usual rent, which was seven thousand) and paid Mr Maple of Maple and Sons another six thousand to furnish and fit out the theatre.

But 1877 was to prove to be Mapleson's worst year yet. Not only was the crisis of the huge building rising beside the Thames becoming unmanageable, but he lost his invaluable soprano, Tietjens. On 28 April she sang Norma, to acclaim; the following day she felt ill, but she struggled back to sing Norma for him once more. Then, on 29 May 1877, she collapsed during a performance of *Lucrezia Borgia*, and on 3 October, although Mapleson was still optimistically announcing her imminent appearance on the Dublin stage as Leonora, she died. It was a dreadful blow: for twenty seasons diva and impresario had worked together. Harold Rosenthal has rated her as 'possibly the greatest dramatic soprano active in the second half of the 19th century', and she had always been there to boost Mapleson's performances, both as a singer and as a friend. He was able to recruit a new star, the Hungarian coloratura soprano Etelka Gerster, who was a demon with her unexpected top Fs; but the death of Tietjens had also encouraged Nilsson to start demanding more money.

By Christmas 1877 the National Opera House was history, but Mapleson was already in New York, finalising his plans for a 'magnificent company', in a city as yet unused to his particular brand of magniloquent semi-success. He was just as capable of pulling off a stupendous *tour-de-force* as of precipitating a total failure: there was just no way of knowing which was to come next. Nor was he often in the secret himself. He just barged forward, no doubt as impressed by his own hyperbole as was everyone else, really meaning every word, and happily drinking in the praise if his schemes worked, or shaking off the criticism if they didn't.

A journeyman impresario, Mapleson was in many ways a perfect example of the opera-as-music-hall school of Schikaneder – whereas he always saw and presented himself as an exemplar in the tradition of Opera-as-Great-Art, and this was a crucial factor in his American adventures.

These got off to a poor start when he had to telegraph for an advance of two thousand pounds from his New York agent, to bail him out of a loss-making tour to Dublin (where he was known as 'Fableson' from his habit of announcing stars in his cast who rarely materialised) and Cork, and even to pay for the ensemble's tickets to America. A charity concert they put on during the crossing raised only four pounds from their fellow-passengers, a sum so low that it was felt necessary to have a company whip-round to add to the total, and avoid embarrassment.

The idea of taking opera to America had originated two years before, at a New Year's Eve Party in 1875, when a guest from New York, the banker August Belmont, told Mapleson he could make a fortune putting on his shows there. He had already been in correspondence with Mapleson, and was adamant that success depended upon the impresario going to New York first and making the arrangements with the greatest

care, and could *only* be assured if he took a top-class company.
It says something for Mapleson's vigour that the next morning
he was up and heading for the port of Queenstown in County
Cork, where he boarded a small Cunard steamer bound for
New York. It took fourteen days to make the crossing, and he
spent the following ten visiting Philadelphia, Chicago, Boston
and Cincinnati.

New York had long offered an uneasy market for opera. Gay's
The Beggar's Opera had been performed at the Nassau Street
Theater in 1750, with modest success. Lorenzo da Ponte,
Mozart's great librettist, had moved to New York, where he
found himself, at the age of 84, backer and manager of the
Italian Opera House, on the corner of Church and Leonard
Streets, when it opened on 18 November 1833 with Rossini's *La
Gazza Ladra*, but this venture ended after two years in financial
collapse.

The only reliable provision of opera came from the Academy
of Music at 14th Street and Irving Place. At the time this was
the largest theatre in the world, holding an audience of over
four and a half thousand; it had been built in 1854 at a cost of
more than three hundred thousand dollars, and opened with
Grisi and Mario in Bellini's *Norma*. A measure of the problems
faced by opera in New York is the fact that from 1854 to 1878,
no management ever produced a second season at the Academy
– until Mapleson, that is.

To escape the humiliating collapse of his Embankment
project, it was to the Academy that Mapleson took his troupe.

Despite what might appear to have been a shaky grasp of
money matters, Mapleson could not have survived this far
without some genuine grasp of financial control. There were
three main sources of income for an impresario: the subscriptions from pre-sold boxes and seats, the daily sales at the box-
office and by street touts, and any financial guarantees against
loss that might be secured from rich devotees. Of these the first
was crucial to cash-flow control, since it was money paid up

front, and enabled a prudent manager to prepare his own budgeted expenditure. With August Belmont as President of the Academy sponsoring his trip, and with the subscriptions lodged to his account (the source of the money he had been able to call upon when he was stranded in Ireland), Mapleson had only to deliver his side of the bargain.

It should not be supposed that Belmont, a shrewd banker, had committed himself without careful thought. Correspondence uncovered by John Cone's meticulous research into the time Mapleson spent in the United States shows that Belmont had assiduously sought references for him. They were not exactly glowing. Bernard Ullman, who had himself produced opera at the Academy, wrote to Belmont on 1 July 1877 saying that Mapleson 'will promise anything very boldly, very well knowing all the time he cannot keep it. You ought to aid him, as much as you can, *mais toujours restant sur vos gardes.*' Baron Ferdinand de Rothschild, a fellow banker, wrote from London that, to quote Cone, 'Mapleson [has] no financial resources and for that reason [I advise] extreme care in any contractual matter.' Ullman wrote again in September: 'Mapleson is very foolish, to announce that he will have new artists in January – he cannot get any – ... he knows it – but such is the man and, in that, he is incorrigible.' Belmont had been fairly warned.

The liner carrying Mapleson and his company steamed into New York harbour a month later, and Mapleson records that their disembarkation was greeted by 'thousands of people, accompanied by military bands'. It was all very gratifying.

Due to open on 16 October with the Hungarian soprano Etelka Gerster as Violetta in Verdi's *La Traviata*, Mapleson called a press conference on the 14th, only to be interrupted in full flow with the news that Gerster was seriously ill with typhoid fever. He rushed off and managed to persuade Minnie Hauk, the young American soprano who had made her début in Brooklyn as Amina, at the age of fourteen, to take the role at short notice – only to find that his Germont *père* immediately withdrew. Again, he was able to persuade a baritone to step in. And all this while his London troupe was due to open the following night at Her Majesty's with *Fidelio*.

Mapleson, at the age of forty-eight, was at the pinnacle of his career. Presenting operas simultaneously in London and New York, he had bounced back with triumph from reverses, miscalculations and misfortunes which might have crushed a lesser man for good. Yet he was still ready to out-face the world. For six months this amazing bonanza continued. Great operas – *The Magic Flute, Faust, Carmen, La Sonnambula* (with Gerster, now fully recovered, as Amina), *Don Giovanni, Lohengrin, Les Huguenots, Rigoletto, Freischütz, Trovatore* – all were rolled out before Mapleson's adoring public. And as a result he was making big money again, despite employing a company of two hundred and forty people in the United States alone.

On they went from New York to Boston, where there were public breakfasts for his singers (those must have been popular); where he met Longfellow; and where the box-office takings for one night, when Gerster sang the title role in *Lucia di Lammermoor*, reached seven thousand dollars. Then on again, a thousand miles west, to Chicago. They travelled in a train equipped with specially decorated rooms, in which Mapleson had his own *salon* and a personal chef, all in return for a total fare of fifteen thousand dollars for a round-trip by way of St Louis, Cincinnati, Philadelphia, Baltimore and Washington.

In Chicago, he spent twenty dollars a night on fuel for braziers to keep the queues at the box-office warm. In the second week, when he put on *I Puritani* starring Gerster, the outer walls began to crack during the course of the performance. The theatre – presumably built of wood – was literally falling apart, and in the office where Mapleson sat working a split opened, wide enough for him to put his hand through it. Only a swift but discreet evacuation of the building avoided a major catastrophe.

Mapleson himself had to be left behind in Chicago, afflicted with gout; but his son Henry, now married to the young soprano Marie Roze, managed the company until his father could rejoin them.

That winter season, from October 1877 to April 1878 Mapleson (or his son) staged a hundred and sixty-four full opera performances and forty-seven concerts, while in England, at the same time, a further hundred and thirty-five operas and forty-eight concerts were presented under his auspices. Nothing like it had ever been attempted before, and since Mapleson's death no one has ever attempted it again.

That autumn also saw the death of Frederick Gye, shot dead in an accident while he was out pheasant shooting with Lord Dillon at Ditchley Park in Oxfordshire. Mapleson, with the memory of his own hideous sporting excursion with the Edinburghs doubtless still vivid in his mind, must have read the news with a certain wry amusement.

Such was his success all round that Mapleson immediately signed a three-year lease at the Academy of Music, no doubt fortified by enthusiastic promises of subscription income; at the same time, he began his preparations – holding auditions, signing contracts – for the ensuing London summer season.

After a brief respite in August, Mapleson was off again. His London and New York autumn seasons were due to open simultaneously on 18 October 1878. In New York, up to his old tricks, Mapleson had managed to squeeze an extra two rows of seats into the stalls in order to boost his income at the expense of the (non-paying) stockholders' comfort.

But again, Madame Gerster was ill. Mapleson engaged other sopranos whom he considered excellent, but something of his reputation for putting on geese in place of the advertised swans had crossed the Atlantic with him, and the New York press began to turn against him.

He sent an urgent summons to Marie Marimon, a reliable French soprano who had sung for him in London and was now based in Paris. Her mother had been drowned at sea, so she was unwilling to risk the Atlantic crossing. Mapleson pleaded; she wavered, and signed her contract; and a much-relieved Mapleson wired her the money, to Rothschilds' bank as she had requested. The situation had, it seemed, been saved – but then Marimon's maid refused to leave her lover in Paris. Apparently she was indispensable to the diva in such an adventure; for good measure she told her mistress she had dreamt that they were all to be drowned at sea.

Marimon cancelled her contract. Mapleson threatened to sue, then tried more persuasive methods. 'Tranquil sea. Charming public. Elegant city. Luxurious living', he cabled; but possibly spoilt his effect by adding desperately: 'For Heaven's sake come, and duplicate your Drury Lane triumphs.'

The box-office receipts began to falter, and Mapleson to despair – whereupon the orchestra went on strike, demanding a ten per cent increase in pay. Mapleson refused, on the grounds that at fifty thousand dollars – their income for the preceding season – their rate was double that of his London players. There was a stand-off, but only half the players turned up for the performance of Donizetti's *Linda di Chamonix* on 29 October. In his *Memoirs* Mapleson claimed the audience were sympathetic when he made an announcement from the stage outlining the problem, but in New York it would have been a sympathy tempered with sceptical disappointment. After all, as they saw it, they were paying him to deliver, not to explain away his failure to do so.

Marimon and her maid finally embarked for New York on *The City of Richmond*. They must have bitterly regretted their decision to do so when a storm in the Atlantic, a hundred and fifty miles from Halifax in Nova Scotia, disabled the ship, breaking the propellor shaft and washing the second officer overboard. They were rescued by the steamer *Circassia* – but Miramon's first action, when she finally reached New York on 29 November, was to hurry to the Catholic Cathedral on 50th Street, when she prostrated herself in thanksgiving for her deliverance. An hour on the icy stone floor caused her to contract a chill so severe that she had to spend the next week in bed. At last, on 3 December, Miramon was well enough to sing in *Sonnambula*; but her condition deteriorated rapidly thereafter, and in the end she was able to sing only a few of her projected performances.

It is a measure of how shaky Mapleson's cash-flow position was at this time that he was briefly made bankrupt in London the following May over a disputed cheque for five hundred pounds in favour of his conductor, Costa. Though the actual bankruptcy only lasted for six minutes, this was a portent of more serious problems which lay in the future.

It was from a position of weakness, therefore, rather than of strength, that Mapleson then negotiated a merger with Ernest and Herbert Gye, the sons of his old adversary. The gist of the arrangement was that Mapleson was to hand over his lease and his trading goodwill in London, plus some of his costumes and scenery, in return for two and a half thousand pounds in cash and ten thousand in shares in the new consortium (to be called The Royal Italian Opera Company (Covent Garden) Limited), plus a three-year contract at a thousand pounds a year plus fifty per cent of the profits from America, where he was to have executive control.

In his *Memoirs*, written ten years later, Mapleson asserts that of course he realised the intention of the younger Gyes was to corner the market for opera in both London and New York. One part of their plan was to stifle Mapleson with easy money; the other was to secure for themselves the management of the new Metropolitan Opera which was rising on a site on the corner of Broadway and 39th Street, the outward and visible sign of the way in which 'new money' (the Vanderbilts, Roosevelts, Morgans and Goulds) was being refused boxes at the Academy, which was very much the preserve of 'old money' (the Belmonts, Astors and Schuylers). With Mapleson having tied up the Academy with his three-year lease, and himself tied up with them by the new contract, the Gyes would have a monopoly on New York opera – or, in other words, a licence to print money.

What is more probable, however, despite his claims to prescience, is that Mapleson was too relieved to be rescued from a second major embarrassment to have seen the whole picture. Others were less distracted, and the new Board of the Metropolitan began quietly to look elsewhere for a manager while maintaining outwardly cordial negotiations with the Gye brothers, as the walls of their building gradually rose on Broadway.

Thus, when Mapleson sailed for New York in October 1881, it was on this occasion less as an impresario than as a partner of the Royal Italian Opera Company (Covent Garden) Limited of London, even though his shares had yet to be issued. And this time his own disembarkation was altogether overshadowed by another imminent arrival, that of Adelina Patti, returning to the city of her birth after an absence of twenty-two years during which she had enjoyed stardom in Europe.

Born in 1843 into a singing family, Patti had fallen early into the Svengali-esque clutches of her Czech brother-in-law (probably also her lover), Maurice Strakosch. Exploited as a child prodigy until she was twelve (Henry James recalled seeing her in a red hussar jacket, 'warbling like a tiny thrush'), she was then retired briefly from touring to develop her voice and improve her technique, until at the age of sixteen she was re-launched as Lucia at the New York Academy of Music, before being taken to London and Paris, where her beauty and poise made her into an immediate star.

Now she had come back, and was expecting to make a fortune from giving recitals on her own account, charging ten dollars a seat. The public, however, whether out of pique at her long absence or from ignorance of her attractions, stayed away, even when the tickets were reduced to two dollars. Mapleson, who had initially worried that she would steal his audiences, saw his chance: he sent her a hundred-dollar bouquet, with the message 'To Adelina Patti, Queen of the Lyric Stage'.

He followed this up by calling on her, expecting to be able to sign her up for the Academy. But he arrived to find that a new adversary had got in ahead of him: Henry Eugene Abbey, fifteen years Mapleson's junior but already a veteran of the promotional tour, had contracted with Patti for a concert tour, on the basis of his own previous success in marketing (or, some said, exploiting) Sarah Bernhardt.

Mapleson, undeterred, managed to secure Patti for the Cincinnati Opera Festival of 1882, but only by offering her sixteen hundred pounds a night, a fee made possible simply because the Music Hall in Cincinnati was capable of providing five thousand seats. Even so, he had to contend with Abbey, who had also managed to sign up Nilsson and was putting on concerts featuring her at the same time as Mapleson's, as a spoiling tactic.

The first night of the Cincinnati Festival opened on 13 February with Meyerbeer's *Les Huguenots*, and ended in disaster when Paolina Rossini, singing Valentine, was hit in the face, quite inexcusably, by flying powder from the firing squad, and then hurt herself further when she fell. While Rossini was being carried away, Mapleson received news that Patti, the star of the second night, had caught cold and would not be able to sing. At least he was able to announce this in good time, and postponed her début until the following Thursday. But she was still unwell, and was again postponed, to the Saturday.

By this time Patti's non-appearance was news all over the United States. Reporters hounded the hotel staff, both where she was staying in Cincinnati and where she had stayed, in Detroit. They discovered that she had bought a bottle of champagne, but their attempts to brand her a drunk were contradicted by her room-waiter, who swore that what little was drunk in Patti's suite was mainly consumed by her 'husband', the tenor Nicolini (Patti was still, legally, the Marquise de Caux, though she had not spoken to her husband for seven years and lived openly with Nicolini).

Even Patti's carriage bill was published, showing that one day when she was supposed to be unwell she had spent fifty-five dollars on being driven round the city. All these details were set against exhaustive interviews with her doctors. Essentially, Patti was subjected to no less press harassment in 1882 than she might have experienced a century later.

Yet all this publicity proved to be good for business, and Mapleson packed in eight thousand people (many of them standing illegally in the aisles) for performances of *Carmen* and *Fidelio*. How his feelings must have fluctuated between relief that his new partners, the Gyes, had made such a success possible, and rage at having to share the profits with them.

This tour took in Detroit, Buffalo, Cleveland, Syracuse and Albany before returning to New York in March. The spring season there featured big productions such as *Lohengrin*, *Les Huguenots*, *William Tell* – and *L'Africaine*, starring Hauk and Campanini, and a full-size elephant powered by two policemen inside it. No wonder 'the Colonel' was compared to Barnum, the circus king; he was even appointed Honorary Colonel attached to New York's 22nd Regiment, in recognition of his military skills.

Where Mapleson really came into his own – and in this field he has had no equal – was in solving the various intense personal dramas that tended to arise during a tour. He clearly relished the challenge, whether it was calming crazed, knife-wielding tenors, mediating between rival gangs of piano porters (Steinway's men, for example, were put to flight by some competitors armed, unimaginatively, with piano legs), or deciding which diva should have which dressing room – this problem he always solved by inventing some special merit for the lesser room, as for example in Dublin, where he asserted that it was the Viceroy's favourite. Indeed, he could show quite remarkable resource. Summoned from dinner (and its freshly-opened pint of champagne) by Gerster's husband, he found her unconscious: she had been treated with chloroform for a sore tooth less than two hours before she was to sing Elsa in *Lohengrin*. His *Memoirs* record a signal restraint: 'I was beside myself, and I am afraid rather rude at the moment to those in attendance.' Rather rude? This was a man with a building full of paying punters, and no understudy.

He threw open the windows, and called for soda water and *sal volatile*. He raised Gerster's head, and applied the smelling salts. No reaction. He picked her up, carried her to his carriage, drove with her to the Academy, and placed her in her dressing room, still unconscious. As she lay slumped over her table he ordered the bemused hairdresser to start plaiting her hair. When Gerster finally woke up, he told her her hair was ready and she should go out on stage. She did.

How many of today's *intendants* would be equal to such demands? Nor, for all their other fine points, is it possible to imagine Sir Thomas Beecham, or John Christie, or even Sir Cameron Mackintosh, coping with such urgent aplomb. Mapleson went back to his dinner and a fresh pint of champagne, confident (and rightly so) that the situation was saved.

His capacity for improvisation was particularly tested the night he was due to present *William Tell* at the Academy. At four in the afternoon he received a doctor's note telling him the prima donna had diphtheria. Just as he was agreeing terms with a substitute, the tenor singing Arnold announced that he too was ill. Mapleson persuaded him to carry on as best he could, but meanwhile the substitute soprano had backed out. Mapleson announced a performance of *Lucia* in place of *William Tell*: Laura Zagury, who had signed to sing it, admitted that she didn't know the role at all yet. He announced *Aïda*: but again, the principal soprano was unwell. *Rigoletto*? Laura Zagury, suffering from the stress of having to admit to not knowing *Lucia*, was far too upset to sing Gilda. *Les Huguenots*? Emmy Fursch-Madi had just taken some medicine. *La Favorite*?

Luigi Ravelli had been rehearsing *Carmen* all day and couldn't sing another note; the only alternative tenor was a member of the chorus so fat that none of the costumes would fit. Of the two possible Leonoras, Hauk was preparing to sing the following night, while Antonia Galassi had boils.

By this time the stage crew, who had been dragging out and pushing back props and scenery like yo-yos, were beginning to flag; and Mapleson's office was occupied by a large deputation from the King of Hawaii, anxious to confer the Royal Order of Kapirlani on Madame Patti.

Mapleson went into over-drive. First he talked the fat tenor into taking on the main role in *La Favorite* by sending for the tailor and having him run up a new costume for him, as they stood there. Then he hurried to Galassi's apartment with the theatre doctor and supervised the immediate lancing of her boils, dragging her to the theatre as the curtain rose, no doubt thanking his stars that Leonora does not appear until Act 2. Finally he took the Royal deputation off to Patti's hotel, where the jewelled star, ribbon and citation were duly presented to the great diva.

No one could have tried harder. But bare-faced cheek and a silver tongue are no substitutes for carefully-rehearsed understudies, and only a few days later Mapleson had to close the theatre on a full house: they had paid to see *Carmen*, but Ravelli refused to get out of bed to sing Don José. Mapleson had had problems casting this role before – when he was mounting *Carmen*'s London première, Campanini had sent the part back, saying he could hardly be expected to take a role with only one love duet, and that with the *seconda donna*. Yet here was Mapleson, in pole position in the richest market for his trade, with no substitute prepared, not even after all the dramas that had already taken place. Was it really that Mapleson did not care? Or was it simply that the music-hall tradition of bodging and winking was too deeply engrained for him to see that times had changed? Either way, it was the wrong way to do business in New York.

When the company reached Baltimore, it was to find that

sales were markedly reduced by a small-pox epidemic. Mapleson had his troupe vaccinated immediately, the singers on their legs, the dancers on their arms. Patti had travelled as far as Philadelphia: there she sat, and simply refused to move.

When they got back to New York, the partners were collecting fourteen thousand dollars (more than six hundred thousand at 1998 rates) from a Patti matinée, and almost as much again from an evening performance of *L'Africaine*. No wonder Mapleson temporarily hid the corpse in a box when a woman died in the rush for seats on the last night. Not even when Herbert Gye was mugged while he was carrying a cheque for Patti in the sum of forty-four hundred dollars was the partners' enthusiasm for their American adventure dimmed. Everything seemed set for the great *coup*: securing control of the Metropolitan as well.

The vast building on Broadway was now up. It had a hundred and twenty-two boxes and seven hundred and thirty-two seats, and its construction had taken three years, and cost nearly one and three-quarter million dollars – almost double the estimate of six hundred thousand for the site and four hundred and thirty thousand for the construction and, for 3,045 seats, roughly the equivalent of fifty-one million dollars at 1998 rates: this compares not unfavourably with the forty-six million dollars it cost to rebuild the Lincoln Center in 1966 with 3,788 seats. The costs were partly financed by the advance sale of fifty-two boxes at ten thousand dollars each, but the money was principally found among the main stockholders, those 'new money' families denied access to the Academy of Music.

Led by Mrs William Vanderbilt, these families were not merely anxious for the social acceptance and position resolutely denied them by the Academy's Old Guard, led by Mrs Henry Astor; they were absolutely determined to achieve them. And with opera at the very heart of social life in New York, as it was in Paris, the very last thing they wanted was a cosy monopoly managed by Mrs Astor's current pets, the far from immaculate Mapleson–Gye junta.

February 1883 found Mapleson at the White House in Washington, putting on a private concert of Mozart, Verdi and Wagner arias with Albani and Sofia Scalchi for President Arthur, then settling down cosily with the Presidential champagne and cigars to hear anecdotes of the great man's early seafaring days. Then it was back to New York, where the Gyes were busying themselves with arrangements, and Mapleson presented *La Traviata* and *Der fliegende Holländer*. Their negotiations with the Board of the Metropolitan seemed to be nearing completion; their plan was about to materialise.

Then came the bombshell. It was announced that the lease of the new Metropolitan Opera House had been granted to Henry Abbey, the same man who had been such a nuisance in previous years, putting on rival concerts in Cincinnati with Nilsson and trying to monopolise Patti's work.

Herbert Gye, believing – and rightly – that he had been strung along by the Vanderbilts, departed for London, leaving his brother and Mapleson to prepare for the coming campaign. Instead of having the opera business of New York and London to themselves, they had now to face major new competition. And while Abbey himself was of no account in the world of opera (being better known as the publicity agent of celebrities like Lily Langtry and Sarah Bernhardt), he had behind him – and was equally well known to have behind him – the bottomless industrially fed wallets of the Vanderbilts, Harrimans, Rockefellers, Drexels and Roosevelts.

Worse was to come. Although she was now theoretically under a new contract to Gye, Abbey announced that Nilsson would continue to sing for him. He offered major fee increases to Campanini and Scalchi, and when a desperate Mapleson, in collaboration with Ernest Gye, agreed to pay Patti the unprecedented fee of four thousand dollars a night, Abbey promptly capped it with an offer of five thousand (at a time when the rate of exchange was five dollars to the pound).

Mapleson and Gye cabled their fellow directors in London,

and all agreed to match Abbey's offer. This Patti accepted, and a contract for a total of fifty thousand pounds was signed by Mapleson on behalf of the Royal Italian Opera Company (Covent Garden) Limited, and by her agent Franchi on behalf of Adelina Patti. Mapleson was reduced to publishing in the *New York Daily Tribune* a letter which he had allegedly sent to Abbey:

If you wish, I will furnish you with a list of those whom I do not propose to engage for next year. This will save your agents a great deal of trouble in waylaying my people outside the stage door, and supplying them with sundry drinks in the neighbourhood while it will enable you to conduct your matters in a more business-like way.

On 28 April, on his way to the liner that was to carry him back to London, Mapleson was serenaded across the harbour by Leopold's Brass Band playing 'Empty Is The Cradle, Baby's Gone' and 'Hail to the Chief'.

Before leaving New York, he had given one final interview, to the *Daily Tribune*. Asked whether he had made any new contracts, he replied:

Yes ... here is a very important one. Print it in full. I have contracted for a special train to be built expressly for the purpose of carrying my opera company around the country. There will be one beautiful palace car for the diva, Madame Patti, and it will be named after her.

Patti's name was his biggest card, and he played it as often as he could.

We have no way of knowing whether Mapleson expected sympathy from his partners, or congratulations. In the event, they threw him out. First, and despite Ernest Gye's involvement in negotiating it, they refused to ratify the Patti contract; then they refused to issue Mapleson his shares. All connection between him and the Gyes was abruptly and shockingly severed.

Having parted with his lease of Her Majesty's Theatre as part of the deal, Mapleson was left holding nothing except the world's most expensive opera contract – for Patti to sing fifty shows for a total of two hundred and fifty thousand dollars – and the contracts of assorted other singers, amounting to a further seventy-five thousand. He also had another two years of his lease of the Academy still to run – rent-free, and with promises of subsidy in return for the stockholders occupying their seats and boxes free of admission charge.

The American Press had been following this drama with great interest, and the Academy stockholders, with whom Mapleson remained surprisingly popular, rescued him by volunteering the forty thousand dollars demanded by Patti as cash up front on her contract. With his main headache reduced and the guaranteed advanced sales income beginning to flow in, Mapleson reverted to what he had always been happiest doing: acting on his own behalf as impresario of his own company.

Abbey had already pinched Nilsson; now he stole Del Puente – who had to pay Mapleson fifteen hundred francs in compensation for breaking his contract to sing for him – Scalchi, Campanini and Fursch-Madi. In a series of unpleasant newspaper interviews, Nilsson now described Mapleson as being 'bald from debauchery' and 'ridiculous', and joked about his absurd use of his honorary colonelcy; Mapleson hit back by declaring that Nilsson's repertoire was now reduced to just four operas and 'Swanee River', and challenged her to name a fifth she could sing. Such petty squabbling notwithstanding, Mapleson still held the ace of trumps, Adelina Patti, along with her faithful Nicolini, Madame Gerster, and the Neapolitan bass Lombardelli.

If Abbey at the Metropolitan Opera had the backing of the Vanderbilts, Mapleson at the Academy had that of Belmont and the Astors. He also enjoyed sudden popularity with the

Musicians' Union: Abbey had imported his orchestra *en bloc* from abroad, and Mapleson records that five hundred members of the Union serenaded him in his hotel the night of his return to New York.

Both houses opened on 22 October 1883, Mapleson with Gerster in his regular stand-by production *La Sonnambula*, and Abbey with *Faust*, starring Nilsson, Campanini, Scalchi and Del Puente – 'a fine cast and perfectly trained, since all these artists had played under my direction and did not even require a rehearsal', as Mapleson notes wryly in his *Memoirs*. To the press, ever happy to print a telling quotation, he said: 'My audience is the Faubourg St-Germain of the town. My rival is supported, I understand, by a number of rich persons who want to find some new way of spending money.'

But it soon became apparent that the attractions of the new building on Broadway, with its spectacular boxes and high standard of artists, were beginning to hit Mapleson's box-office takings. He was charging between six hundred and eight hundred dollars for a six-seater box for thirty nights, and from four hundred to five hundred for four-seaters. Single stalls were a hundred and twenty-five dollars the season, and seats in the balcony eighty dollars. At the Metropolitan, which then seated about three thousand, Abbey was renting boxes for fifteen hundred dollars, for the season.

Mapleson called a meeting with the Academy directors, and warned them that without additional subsidy, his troupe (lately renamed Her Majesty's Opera Company) would fold. The directors offered him twenty-five thousand dollars (in effect, just five nights of Patti – who had yet to arrive), and this was underwritten by the Bank of the Metropolis on condition that Mapleson did not draw more than three thousand of it in any one week.

Abbey continued with *Lucia, I Puritani, Mignon, Lohengrin, Don Giovanni* and *Carmen*, which represented a dream season for the New York audiences when combined with Mapleson's *Rigoletto*,

Norma, *Il Trovatore*, *Lucia* (again), *Faust*, *Martha* and *Linda di Chamonix*. For the first time in New York, lovers of opera must have felt themselves spoilt for choice … until poor performances began to threaten Mapleson's credibility.

His second *Rigoletto*, on 24 October, had Bertini, a new young tenor, singing the Duke at the alarmingly early age of twenty-six. This would have been possible in the Fenice perhaps; at the larger Academy, with its more challenging acoustics, surely not. He cracked badly in '*La donna è mobile*', and then his attempt on the top B-flat in the Quartet produced audible laughter from the stalls. The *Herald* held that 'it is sheer impertinence to bring such people to America', while the *Evening Post* suggested helpfully that Bertini 'would make a good end man for the chorus'.

Mapleson paid him off, under protest, after the tenor's lawyers froze Mapleson's bank account. This was not the moment for him to risk a major law-suit, and Bertini sailed back to Europe. Only two days later Marie Pappenheim, his Norma, sounded forced, and both she and the tenor got poor reviews; as did the whole production, for being under-rehearsed.

Then Mapleson's *Faust*, given on 2 November with a completely new cast (since his regulars were all at the Metropolitan on Broadway) was generally agreed to be a complete disaster, especially when compared with the new version at the Met. Abbey, meanwhile, was spending lavishly on artists and costumes alike (all his costumes and shoes were sent over from Worth, the ultra-chic Lincolnshire-born Parisian couturier first championed by the Empress Eugénie), and achieving high standards. He was soon seen to be winning the duel between the impresarios, although there was gossip that he was haemorrhaging money at the rate of fifteen thousand dollars a week, and that the Met.'s acoustics were very poor.

These weeks must have been a time of sad worry for the normally ebullient showman as he waited impatiently for the arrival of Patti, his one big gun. At last she was due. Mapleson hired sixteen tugs to trumpet her arrival, while massed military bands assembled overnight on the quayside; Arditi, at the head of the opera chorus and orchestra, wrote a special cantata; and the enterprising Colonel even suborned some artillery for a twenty-one-gun salute. Considering the trouble everyone had taken, it seems a pity that Patti's ship should have passed all this by in the fog and landed her, alone and unwelcomed, at a different dock altogether, where she had to struggle to find a cab to get to her hotel.

On 9 November, before an Academy audience of New York's *ancien régime*, Patti came on stage, as Ninetta in Rossini's *La Gazza ladra*, to be met with a full five minutes' ovation. Afterwards, she was judged to have sung as brilliantly as they had all expected. But that was it; the rest of the cast, the production, even the piece itself were judged old-fashioned, under-rehearsed, and well below the new standard set by the Met.

What Mapleson needed now was a second and more convincing blockbuster performance by Patti. She was due to sing Violetta on 12 November; instead, she announced that she had a cold, and for four long days she remained out of sight, prompting strong rumours that she was about to defect to the Met.

Then on 16 November she sang Violetta, on the 19th she sang Lucia, on the 23rd Elvira in Verdi's *Ernani*, and on the 28th her first American Aïda. All these performances were greeted with wild enthusiasm, and filled the house. There was no doubt about it: she was earning her colossal fees.

Abbey, alarmed by Patti's success, offered her six thousand dollars a performance, plus forty thousand on top for her to pay off Mapleson with if he tried to enforce her contract. On 4 December the *New York Herald* quoted Mapleson as describing this offer as 'an unexampled piece of villainy'.

There was also trouble brewing within the company. Etelka Gerster was twenty-eight, and she it was who almost single-handedly had kept Mapleson's show alive until Patti's late arrival; but she was being paid only a thousand dollars a performance, and was beginning to suffer emotionally from the excessive idolatry shown to her older colleague. Their repertoires overlapped, since both were singing Lucia, Linda, Harriet, and Marguerite for Mapleson, and that in itself was bound to become a source of friction. In Philadelphia, seeing Patti's name advertised in larger letters than her own, Gerster had stormed out and taken the next train back to New York. Mapleson had managed to have her train stopped at Wilmington, where the southbound train had been held so that the fleeing diva could be brought back in time for the show. By great ill-fortune Patti was in the latter train, and predictably furious about being delayed because of her rival's tantrums. Unsurprisingly, perhaps, nothing would induce Gerster to board a train containing Patti. Mapleson had to change the advertised opera, which resulted in a third of his audience walking out; he then had to take the night train to New York, to find Gerster and persuade her to return to Philadelphia.

By now even Mapleson was beginning to feel aggrieved by Patti's demands. Every afternoon before a performance, her agent Franchi would appear beside Mapleson, ready to receive the five-thousand-dollar fee in cash. When the harrassed impresario could only produce four thousand (itself an enormous sum) in receipts from the box-office, Franchi immediately left, announcing that the whole contract was thereby annulled.

After Mapleson had had an hour or so to think about this Franchi came back, and congratulated him on his good luck in having so generous a friend as Patti: she had decided not to break the contract, and would come to the theatre – but she would not begin to dress for the show until the missing thousand dollars was handed over. Eight hundred dollars from late ticket sales persuaded her to put on everything but her shoes, and Mapleson somehow managed to scrape together the last two hundred dollars, whereupon Patti swept happily onto the stage and gave a magnificent performance.

Patti's costumes, indeed, were an important item in her

armoury. Part of the fortune she amassed from Mapleson and his rivals was invested in massive jewels, and these were sewn into her personal dresses, so that she sparkled and glistened like a fairy goddess in the flickering gas lamps that lit the stage. But her greed cooled even Mapleson's ardour for her voice. On a good night he was clearing just twenty-two dollars for himself, but more than that (he says), he minded the fact that finer artists, such as Mario, and his dead friend Tietjens, had felt themselves well rewarded with a twentieth of what Patti exacted.

So why did he pay? He must by now have been terrified of a further taste of defeat. There had been too many: first the National Opera House on the Embankment, then the near-disaster of his second American tour and his brief bankruptcy in London, and finally, being booted out of his partnership. Mapleson was a man who thrived on the rich drama of grand opera – even if he did rarely watch one of his own performances throughout – but he had not enough self-esteem to keep him from shrinking at the thought of another total and public failure. Yet such a failure was only days away, *but for Patti*. It was she who kept everything afloat, with the income from her sales (seven dollars per seat, gross, for her nights, as against five dollars for Gerster's), the magic of her name, which could be used to satisfy creditors and subscribers, the public hysteria that she generated when she appeared (a double-edged sword, this – the second time she failed to appear in Detroit, the disappointed crowd threatened to demolish the theatre).

No matter that she (or, more probably, the shrewd Nicolini) had evidently calculated that Abbey would not accede to her outrageous demands for cash up front (as it was often paid in notes or gold coin, the sheer bulk must have been difficult to arrange, and a dangerous invitation to theft); and, further, that the rumours of Abbey's overspending might be true, which meant a risk that his bigger offers might never be paid. Of course she was better off with the abject Mapleson – but of course he could not see clearly enough to realise this.

So Mapleson laboured on to meet Patti's demands, and she continued to build up her great fortune in diamonds and real estate. She gave several powerful performances in New York before the whole company embarked on Mapleson's famous train, with its eleven carriages plus Mapleson's own coach and, bringing up the rear, Patti's private palace on wheels. They steamed eastwards towards Chicago, only to find Abbey's Metropolitan company already there; and, what was almost worse, actually staying in the same hotel, the Grand Pacific.

Mapleson put a good face on the hotel *contretemps* by commenting that surely 'such a galaxy of talent had never been congregated together under one roof', and opened with Patti giving her Annetta, followed the second night by Gerster singing Adina in Donizetti's *L'Elisir d'amore*. Then on the third night he marshalled all his forces and presented *Les Huguenots* with Patti as Valentine and Gerster as Marguerite de Valois.

Tickets were changing hands in the street for twenty-five dollars, and *The Chicago Daily Tribune* described *Les Huguenots* as 'by far the most sensational opera performance that ever occurred in Chicago'. Back-stage shared in the sensation, as relations between Patti and Gerster continued to sour.

It was, and remains, common practice for admirers, family, lovers, even the impresario, to send huge bouquets to their favourite diva, to be presented on stage at an appropriate moment. In Patti's case, her agent Franchi usually stage-managed their appearance, but on this particular night he was away.

At the first interval the applause was for Gerster, who had already sung extensively, while Patti's character had scarcely yet appeared. The footmen, however, brought on all the bouquets – none for Gerster but a great many for Patti. Each time the footmen came on, the crowd's expectation was that the next flourish of roses must surely be for Gerster, standing there with empty arms; but each time they were for the over-loaded Patti. The audience began to display an unaccustomed impatience, and a small offering finally brought on for Gerster elicited a disproportionate roar of appreciation. Patti stormed off-stage, swearing never to sing with Gerster again. The more she thought about the ridiculous position she had been put in, the more enraged she became, and by the end of the show she was hysterical. Back at the hotel she threw herself onto the floor of her room, kicking and screaming. Mapleson records that they all had the greatest difficulty in getting her to bed, and that she blamed him for the whole fiasco.

But if Mapleson was suffering, Abbey, against all expectations, was on his last legs. With the Vanderbilts' blank cheques and his own fortune, he had put together a world-class company from scratch. He had the most expensive costumes ever assembled, he had splendid scenery. However, he was trained more as a publicist than as an opera impresario, and in the end he proved to lack the sheer momentum needed to maintain high standards.

On 14 February Mapleson opened at Minneapolis with *La Sonnambula*, and that day's *New York Times* published the first season's accounts of the Metropolitan Opera Company. They had lost nearly a quarter of a million dollars and Abbey, their manager/lessor, had personally lost a further estimated six hundred thousand of his own. He was effectively wiped out. This was news which must have brought some encouragement to the battered Mapleson as he travelled to St Louis with a company whose two main singers would not perform together.

The rivalry between the divas was in no way diminished when it was reported that the State Governor, Thomas Crittenden, had called on Patti and, in the heat of the moment, kissed her. In the ensuing furore, he claimed he had been encouraged by hearing that she had kissed some schoolgirls. Patti herself made light of it, telling reporters: 'Well, he kissed me ... a nice-looking old gentleman ... what can I do?' Gerster was equally dismissive. When asked for her opinion, she remarked: 'I don't see anything in that to create so much fuss.

There's nothing wrong in a man kissing a woman old enough to be his mother.'

Relations between Patti and Gerster were now at breaking point. As Mapleson prepared for the company to make what would be an epic journey across the continent to San Francisco, Gerster announced that she would only go if Patti did not.

Mapleson, feeling that he could no longer afford Patti, and comfortably aware that Abbey was now safely out of the contest, agreed. The company prepared themselves to board the train for Denver, Colorado at two in the morning, whereupon Gerster – entirely predictably, in the light of her previous success with that dangerous weapon, the ultimatum – suddenly decided that after all she would not be going. Patti, no doubt mourning the loss of those stupendous fees, sent Mapleson a gracious note to say that *she* would be only too happy to accompany him to the Far West. Having gratefully accepted this offer he went along to Gerster's room, only to find her already dressed and ready to embark, having again changed her mind.

The upshot of these vacillations was that *both* divas reached Denver, where Gerster sang Amina and Patti Violetta. Gerster's decision to leave the company revived, but she was mollified by Mapleson's assurance that Patti was only there 'just in case'. This seems to have been the first occasion on which Mapleson discovered, rather late in his career, the extraordinary psychological power of having an understudy on hand.

The company gave *Sonnambula* in Cheyenne, where they were greeted by the band of the US 9th Infantry, brought in from a nearby fort. It was just six years since General Custer had died at the head of the 7th Cavalry at Little Big Horn, since Wild Bill Hickok had been shot in a Deadwood saloon. Billy The Kid had been finally hunted down two years earlier, and Wyatt Earp was still a young man. This was a pioneering trip by any standards. They were passing through the Old West, as recreated by John Ford on film. These were unruly frontier communities to whom the railroad was bringing the promise, and the trade, of a new civilisation. Nevertheless, Mapleson sold eight hundred tickets in Cheyenne, at the colossal price of ten dollars each.

Next they gave *Lucia di Lammermoor* in Salt Lake City. Here Mapleson, stirred by the sight of the Mormons' twelve thouand-seater Tabernacle, which for religious reasons was out of bounds for secular performances, encouraged Patti to entertain the Prophet, John Taylor, and his twelve 'Apostles' to dinner in her sumptuous railway-carriage. Her coach had cost sixty thousand dollars. It had its own white and gold salon, complete with painted ceiling and two-thousand-dollar Steinway piano, and its own dining section; it had rolled-gold lamps, silk damask curtains and gilded tapestried ceilings; it had a solid silver bath; even its key was fashioned in eighteen-carat gold.

Asked in return to visit the Tabernacle, Patti contrived to mention what a wonderful acoustic it had. Mapleson chimed in, saying it was the perfect place for a concert. The Prophet seemed to be taken with the idea, but the Apostles objected.

Patti sang a little, she enquired closely into the Mormon religion; she even indicated an interest in joining. From then on, the only disagreement centred on whether tickets should be two dollars or three – three dollars was deemed to be too much to expect a man with five wives to pay – and a tentative date was fixed for their return on the way back from San Francisco, where they were due to open with Gerster singing Lucia on 10 March.

When the train stopped at Reno to take on water, it was boarded by reporters, all interested only in interviewing Patti. At Truckee they found the line had been washed away by an avalanche of snow from the mountains, and was being repaired by a massive gang of Chinese workmen. There were Red Indians everywhere now, and Patti had to be forcefully dissuaded by Nicolini from adopting one of their papooses, who showed a particular penchant for laughing at her. At Sacramento, crowds of Indians and Chinese besieged her car, apparently anxious to hear her sing.

When they finally reached Oakland in California, Patti bought the morning papers. Seeing that the announced programme did not include her, she of course demanded angrily to know why she had been brought three thousand miles to no purpose. Mapleson was in a dilemma. He knew that nearly seventy per cent of his tickets were already sold. He had promised Gerster that Patti would not sing, yet Patti was the only person the San Francisco audience was interested in.

He found an ingenious solution: he placed an advertisement in the paper to the effect that, as Patti and Nicolini were in the city, he had persuaded them to give a concert – for tickets to which those who had previously bought his opera tickets would have priority.

Gerster accepted this compromise (perhaps she had been fearing worse), and tickets for Patti's performances sold out instantly. The queue for the concert started at ten o'clock the night before. Men camped out with cigars and whisky, and some people even sold their place in the queue for as much as twenty dollars.

The company stayed at William Sharon's spectacular Palace Hotel, one of the wonders of the Western seaboard. Its glass-domed courtyard was surrounded by six tiers of grand galleries, and Patti was serenaded there the first night by a local orchestra.

Indeed, the whole of San Francisco presented a spectacle of conspicuous, spendthrift extravagance: at the Opera, on Mission Street, crystal fountains ran with *eau-de-cologne*, and the hallway was smothered in orchids, violets and roses. The scent must surely have been over-powering. Opera had been a popular feature in the city ever since an itinerant troupe of Italians, the Pellegrinis, first arrived by wagon train and performed *La Sonnambula* on 24 January 1851.

Gerster opened with a highly successful Lucia, but Patti-mania produced a backlash. When the news spread that Patti was to sing Violetta, an enormous queue formed at the Opera box-office. Mapleson's manager opened for business, supposedly with four hunded tickets still available, but promptly closed again, claiming to be sold out, after selling twenty-five tickets to the first five in the queue. In fact, the remaining tickets had clearly been passed to the touts, who were unconstrained by the publicised prices and were asking a hundred dollars for a twenty-five-dollar box and ten dollars for seats with a face value a quarter of that. The touts were poised to make a killing.

The public rebelled. Mapleson denied being in any way involved, but all the San Francisco papers condemned him for sharp practice. He brushed the incident aside in his *Memoirs*, but it certainly tarnished his reputation in San Francisco. The Opera had seats for more than two thousand, but four thousand crammed into the building. There were fights between people with duplicate tickets, and one man challenged another to fight it out in a gun-duel in the street. A gang-plank had been erected across from a neighbouring building, enabling more and more to smuggle themselves in unchecked.

Crowley, the city's Chief of Police, could do nothing that night, as any attempt to clear the theatre would have led to a major riot and almost certainly loss of life. Mapleson disclaimed all responsibility – it was not, after all, his theatre, and he had no physical control over who was allowed in – but nevertheless Crowley threatened him with prosecution, and indicted him the next morning.

That night, however, was Patti's. She had diamonds in her hair, diamonds round her neck and wrists, diamonds dangling from her ears and stitched into her clothes. The audience loved her. Her unorthodox private life, her beauty, her jewels, above all her incandescent reputation – all this was as a powerful drug to San Francisco, the city that had risen from shanty town to major metropolis in less than forty years. The railroad had only reached it in 1869, but Californians already knew they had arrived and, basking in what their new-mined gold and silver could buy, they recognised in Patti the apogee of hard-nosed success.

No one cared that the older-established social leaders of the city were inclined to prefer Gerster to a flagrant adulteress, or for the *San Francisco Chronicle's* acidulated comment that Patti had 'become a spectacle, like Jumbo or any other freak, and the world goes to see rather than to hear ... La diva treated the house to a view of as many of her diamonds as she could carry on without being brought in on trestles.'

The next day after lunch Mapleson was arrested for violating Section 49 of the City's Fire Ordinance, the penalty for which included not less than six months' imprisonment. For the job of trying to keep him out of jail at least until the opera season was over he promptly hired the egregious General W. H. L. Barnes, the controversial star of the hotelier William Sharon's current divorce case, one of the longest-running and most vitriolic domestic battles of nineteenth-century America.

Meanwhile Lombardelli, Mapleson's Neapolitan bass, died suddenly of pneumonia on 17 March. It became known that, in a subscription raised among the cast for his impoverished widow, Mapleson gave six hundred dollars, Patti a hundred and fifty, Nicolini a hundred, and Gerster a munificent thousand dollars. Those who were socially championing Gerster felt thoroughly vindicated.

On 21 March, despite all General Barnes's efforts in demanding further delays – for a jury, for more time for evidence, for himself, as being too busy with the Sharon case, for anything that would keep his client out of jail – Mapleson was brought before Judge Webb, who found him guilty, but allowed him to settle his statutory fine of seven hundred and fifty dollars in opera tickets.

Then, on 25 March, as Mapleson sat in his room on the fourth floor of the Palace Hotel, complacently counting up several thousand pounds-worth of dollars, 'the atmosphere suddenly became dark. A sort of wind was blowing round the apartment, and my senses seemed to be leaving me. The hotel rocked three inches one way and then three inches another.'

Everything – cutlery, money, ornaments – cascaded onto the floor. Mapleson, realising it was an earthquake, scrambled for the door, and ran downstairs, to encounter the imperturbable William Sharon on his way in from the street:

'Don't be frightened,' he said.
'Well, but I am.'
'Nonsense! My hotel is earthquake-proof as well as fire-proof,' he said, handing me a card on which I found this inscribed: 'The Palace Hotel. Fire-proof and earthquake-proof.'

Everything in the hotel was made of wood or iron, and it had four miles of malleable iron wound round it. Sharon said that it might move into another street, but could not fall down. (He was right: in the great earthquake of 1906, the hotel stood undamaged. But this was a Pyrrhic victory, since it was then entirely consumed in the fires which followed.)

Despite this alarm, Patti sang that night, bringing Mapleson twenty-five thousand dollars in ticket income against her five-thousand-dollar fee. When the company's train steamed away from San Francisco on its way back East, he calculated that he had taken more than two hundred thousand dollars from the seventeen nights there.

In Salt Lake City, they found the Prophet had been busy: a new railroad line had been laid to the door of the Tabernacle. Fourteen thousand people attended the concert, and again Mapleson took twenty-five thousand dollars. Not for the first time, Patti was proving that a world-class star can demand record fees, and still leave the management a handsome profit.

In Omaha the company gave *Lucia di Lammermoor*, with Gerster, but they cancelled their visit to Cincinnati, where severe flooding had provoked riots and barricades: the prison and the Court House had been burned down, and the National Guard had had to open fire upon the crowds.

When they got back to New York, Scalchi and Del Puente returned to the company, and Mapleson even went so far as to make discreet overtures towards Nilsson, no doubt with an eye to the future. Patti gave a final performance on 14 April with Nicolini, in *Romeo and Juliet.* She sailed back to Europe on the *Oregon*, and the rest of the company left the next day ... without Mapleson.

The Bank of the Metropolis had attached all his receipts from the final Patti performance, and indeed all his property, including his scenery and costumes at the Academy. The Bank had underwritten the twenty-five thousand dollars of additional subsidy Mapleson had negotiated from Belmont and the Academy stock-holders when he was under pressure from Abbey the previous October, and now it wanted its money back.

As far as Mapleson was concerned, the subsidy had been guaranteed by Belmont and his colleagues, in order to keep their opera season from falling apart. He expected them to pay. But the guarantors had been reading in the newspapers about Mapleson's great financial bonanza on tour, and were not prepared to pay up for someone who was making thousands in profit on guarantees which had been negotiated as being against loss.

To Mapleson, these two concepts were far apart. On the one hand there was his New York season, undertaken and continued only through the extra support he had been promised. What might or might not have happened out West was an altogether separate matter (and, he considered, the icing on the cake). Negotiations were not at all improved by the Metropolitan camp's public statement that they had no problems about paying up on any guarantees made on *their* behalf, and their sententious conclusion, that if you wanted good opera, of course you had to pay for it.

In the end Mapleson won, but at a cost. Belmont resigned from the Presidency of the Academy of Music; his place was taken by Augustus Brown, a reluctant figurehead drafted in by his colleagues, and Mapleson had to leave New York without any firm arrangement having been made for the autumn season. The *New York Tribune* of 18 May printed his parting words from the quayside: 'If anyone says I'm not coming back, don't believe a word of it. Mapleson may die, but he never surrenders. God bless you!' In his *Memoirs*, however, he confides that he was 'very glad to get out of the place'.

Mapleson sailed back to England with a variety of gifts, including the gold watch and chain and the diamond studs and cuff-links he had been presented with on stage on the company's last night at the Academy. It is also likely that he bore with him the considerable profits from San Francisco and Salt Lake City. But somewhere along the thousands of miles of land and sea between San Francisco and London, something had changed. Where before he had charm, now it rang false; where there had been a combative fervour, now there was rancour; where cheerful insouciance, now a morbid refusal to listen. It was as if reaching the age of fifty-four changed him suddenly from a cheerful, incorrigible imp into a bitter old man. And the effect of this on his business was dire.

This new and unwelcome mood makes its first appearance in his *Memoirs* early in the second volume, in a passage of bitter reflections on Patti's greed. After three hundred pages of gush, in which every soprano is 'a songbird of rare talent' and every performance 'a triumph *par excellence*', it is alarming, and a considerable shock, to hear a sudden snarl from the honey-comb.

The position of the Academy stockholders, who now had to decide how to deal with their recalcitrant tenant, was this: in effect they owned the building, and their return (in lieu of the interest or dividends they would have received had they invested their capital differently) lay in their free occupation and enjoyment of their boxes and seats at whatever entertainment took place on their premises. If opera was presented, their dividend was seeing the opera free, instead of having to buy seats like everyone else.

There was therefore a compelling logic to agreeing to a 'subsidy' if that resulted in, for instance, a much more desirable (which is to say, more valuable) performance, one for which in the absence of their entitlement they would in any event have been prepared to pay more. And if no performances took place (as had seemed likely to be the case if Mapleson had gone under the previous autumn), then their right to attend would have been rendered worthless, at least temporarily.

But Brown and his fellow directors had been seriously offended by Mapleson's public abuse of them in the newspapers, and it was not easy for any of them to bring themselves to agree terms that entailed giving him anything; they had come to dislike him intensely. Mapleson, on the other hand, who was lucky to have escaped bankruptcy, and on whom the whole trading burden fell, would clearly be unable to engage new singers for the traditional New York autumn season without having some idea of what extra resources might be available to him.

While the Academy remained silent, the Met.'s ultra-smart new Board Secretary, E. C. Stanton, announced that they were offering a subsidy of seventeen hundred dollars per show for fifty-two performances to (of all people) Ernest Gye to take over from Abbey. They had not found it difficult to refuse the far from attractive offer made them in desperation by Abbey – that he would run their second season if they would pay off his personal debts from the first. This generous guarantee by the Met. must have seemed like a double blow to Mapleson – his own supposed supporters ignoring him, and his hated erstwhile partner Gye offered everything on a plate at the Met. He continued to make matters worse by publicly complaining about the Academy.

In early July he wrote to the directors claiming that for a guarantee of just fifty thousand dollars he could supply both Patti and (despite his vitriolic exchanges with her only the previous year) Nilsson. There was no reply. He began to talk in terms of just putting on concerts during the final year of his lease on the Academy, rather than full-scale opera performances.

But then, on 23 July, it was announced that his former partners, the Royal Italian Opera Company (Covent Garden) Limited, had gone into liquidation (the music critic of the *Sunday Times*, Hermann Klein, partly blamed Emma Albani, still one of the principal sopranos at Covent Garden, for exercising too much control over her husband, Ernest Gye) and that Gye, himself in danger of going bankrupt, was unable to take up the Met.'s offer. With just three months to go before their anticipated season was due to open, and with the threat of their three and a half million dollar investment lying silent, the Met. directors began to panic.

On 14 August they announced that Dr Leopold Damrosch, a German immigrant and conductor of the New York Symphony Society, was taking over – but as an employee, with a salary of eight thousand dollars plus a profit-sharing scheme. They were, in effect, taking on the risks of presenting opera themselves, instead of leasing out the building to a professional impresario. The announcement went on to note that the forthcoming season would concentrate on German opera.

Finally the Academy stockholders met. However much they had come to dislike Mapleson, there was nothing to be gained by keeping their building dark, and if he was serious about not putting on opera there, they risked losing the whole point of their own investment. A hundred and seventeen of the two hundred entitled to vote attended the meeting, and a reasonable majority (eighty-six) supported sending Mapleson the following letter:

The conditions are [for offering a thirty-thousand-dollar subsidy] that either Mme Patti or Mme Nilsson shall appear on each of these nights, and that Colonel Mapleson shall only be allowed the assessment for representations in which Mme Patti or Mme Nilsson shall take part. The assessment is to be paid to the Executive Committee, and at the close of each week that body will hand over to Colonel Mapleson the amount due to him for the performances given by Mmes Patti and Nilsson.

As Mapleson tells the tale in his *Memoirs*, this was a blanket offer of thirty thousand dollars – further evidence of his almost wilful refusal to read a contract.

In any case, Mapleson's relations with his divas had deteriorated. Nilsson flatly refused to join his company; Mapleson claims that she had decided to rest, but a more likely explanation is that she refused to work for him again. John Cone's researches have thrown up a letter from Patti dated 24 September 1884, now in the Pierpont Morgan Library, in which she refers to Mapleson as 'this fool of a worm', complaining that he had dared to dictate to her. Nevertheless she did sign up for the season, at her usual five thousand dollars a night, claiming that this, her twenty-fifth season in America, would also be her last – but, in true operatic fashion, she was still giving regular farewell performances thirty years later.

Mapleson's ensemble now included Scalchi, Nicolini, his conductor Arditi, and a potential new American star, Emma Nevada, who had been studying in Vienna but had first sung for Mapleson in London four years before. The impresario and his company reached New York on 2 November. He immediately began publicly to rubbish the idea of 'sauerkraut opera', but also to grumble about the Academy.

Indeed, Mapleson now had some real grounds for complaint: he found that the directors had been busily sub-letting the Academy space to other companies for rehearsals – including even the Met. As a result, he was seriously hampered in fixing his own rehearsal schedule, perfunctory though it no doubt was.

Then, on 17 November, as Mapleson gave *La Favorite* at the Academy, the Met., newly regilded and redecorated under the directorship of Leopold Damrosch, opened with *Tannhäuser*.

This was followed by *Fidelio, Les Huguenots* (sung in German), *Lohengrin* and *Der Freischütz*. Sauerkraut opera had definitely arrived, and was proving very popular.

One of Mapleson's persistent complaints about the Academy was that its patrons included a small clique, 'the masked conspirators', who were closet Metropolitan supporters, doing their best to undermine him. But this was only half-true.

The love of opera is very often allied to its ambience, and especially to the concept of 'society'. Opera managers and critics complain of this in the same way that others complain of businessmen in restaurants. However, where opera, or fine food, is made available *because* of the income brought in or generated by aspiring socialisers or financiers, there is a case to be made for thanking these contributors, rather than abusing them.

Certainly it was a major part of the rationale of the Academy stockholders that 'their' opera performances should also be, and be seen as, social events – and the summer's uncertainties had persuaded a number of them to extend a stealthy foot into the rival camp, to be ready for a quick switch if that should prove advisable. For as long as 'old New York' could maintain a fine front at the Academy, that was still the place to be, and to be seen, especially if you did not like German opera. But if the Academy was in danger of slipping, it was clear that the Met. would immediately take its place: it was well to be prepared, and there were therefore a number of Academy stockholders who now had boxes at the Met. as well. However, it is undoubtedly fair to say that the troubles between them and Mapleson were largely caused by his new obstreperousness, rather than by their 'disloyalty'.

Emma Nevada made her American début at the Academy on 24 November as Amina, and risked serious *lèse-majesté* by singing 'Home, Sweet Home', Patti's signature tune, as an encore. Her studies in Vienna had been undertaken to help her rather light voice grow, and there had also been worries about her stamina. That night all was well, however, and she got excellent reviews.

On 26 November Mapleson held a Silver Jubilee celebration of Patti's twenty-five years at the Academy, which included a performance of Flotow's *Martha*. Patti had made her début at the Academy at the age of sixteen, singing Lucia – one of the rare occasions when that role can have been sung by someone of the same age as the character. We have two eye-witness accounts of the Silver Jubilee performance, and they could hardly contradict one another more. Mapleson wrote:

> The jubilee performance was a brilliant success ... she was afterwards recalled innumerable times ... at the close of the opera a carriage with four milk-white steeds which I had arranged for was standing to convey its precious burthen to her hotel. Following this we had 100 torchbearers, for the most part admirers and supporters of the opera. Mounted police were on either side of Patti's carriage. At the end of the procession was a waggon full of people letting off Roman candles and large basins of powder ...

Henry Krebhiel, on the other hand, in his *Chapters on Opera*, wrote:

> *Martha* was performed in a manner wholly commonplace in all respects except as to the titular role [Patti]. There was only a little perfunctory applause but Colonel Mapleson had resolved that the scene should be enacted, of which we have often read, in which devotees of the prima donna unhitch the horses from her carriage and themselves drag it, with wild rejoicings, through the streets. To make sure of such a spontaneous ovation in staid New York was a question which Mapleson solved by hiring fifty or more Italians ... As a demonstration it was the most pitiful affair I have ever witnessed. In fact it seemed to me such a humiliation of the great artist that I suggested ... that something adequate and appropriate to so interesting an anniversary be arranged.

Unfortunately, Krebheil's chosen celebration proved a further humiliation for Patti. A banquet to be held in her honour at the Hotel Brunswick had to be hastily reorganised as a men-only affair when it became apparent that the society wives of New York would not consent to dine with a woman living flagrantly in sin, no matter whether it was her Silver, Gold or even Centenary Jubilee.

At this point, Nevada more or less withdrew from performing. Throughout his career, Mapleson had a questionable habit of announcing that one star or another would sing a part that either they did not know, or for which their voice was manifestly unsuited. No doubt he did this to fill awkward gaps in his company, feeling that the singers in question would accommodate him as best they could. Some did, others refused. On one occasion he actually sued a tenor for refusing to sing Elvino, on the grounds that any self-respecting tenor should have the part in his repertoire.

Nevada had had problems with her health and with her voice, and by announcing without consultation that she was to sing Gilda on 3 December, Mapleson managed to exacerbate both. That afternoon he announced that she could not sing after all, as she was tired from her long sea-voyage. Nevada then gave a press conference at which she announced that she could perfectly well sing, but not Gilda (a much heavier role than its main aria might suggest). Mapleson promptly announced her to sing Gilda on the 6th, then reluctantly changed this to Lucia, which she then sang. He announced her again as Gilda, on the 10th. She cancelled because of ill-health, and also missed singing Amina in Brooklyn the following night. Mapleson threatened to sue her – a pointless gesture, since any singer can withdraw because of illness. He was beginning to lose his touch with his singers, as well as with his clients. Not only had he seriously upset Nevada, but the public, losing confidence in his announcements, began to stay away.

On 23 December, giving evidence for Scalchi in a lawsuit

against Abbey (for withholding other payments already due as damages for loss arising from her non-appearance consequent upon his financial collapse), Mapleson was asked whether it was usual for an operatic management to close a theatre just because the prima donna would not appear. His answer – 'It is not ... I think by deliberately closing the theatre Mr Abbey pulled his nose at the expense of his face' – could as well have been directed at himself. Evidence of his increasingly tenuous hold on reality came when he announced the next day that he was considering the formation of a consortium to build a new opera house at Madison Square.

Everything changed when he left New York. Now that Abbey was off the circuit, and with the Met. making only brief visits to Boston and Philadelphia, Mapleson had the rest of the United States to himself. As has been amply demonstrated both before and since, the one certain way to make money from opera is to combine two things: a good company, and a monopoly.

In Boston, Philadelphia, New Orleans (where part of the ceiling fell during Patti's last act, causing a rapid exit by the audience in the stalls), St Louis, Kansas City, Topeka, St Joseph, Cheyenne and Salt Lake City (which his old friend the Prophet had had to leave in a hurry, because of problems with the Inland Revenue Service), Mapleson's opera had no competition, and therefore met with enthusiastic support.

Although Nevada had been giving sporadic performances of Lucia and Amina, she was still ailing either in voice or in temper. When the company finally reached San Francisco Miss Nevada, now in her home state, had not sung for a month, while Patti, Scalchi and the redoubtable Emma Fursch-Madi had had to work doubly hard to fill the gap. Mapleson became increasingly frustrated by Nevada's megaphone diplomacy, which took the form of public statements issued by her manager (and husband), Dr Palmer.

'All the news from her,' complained Mapleson to the *San Francisco Chronicle* on 18 March,

is received at second hand. The public all knows before I do
… I read with surprise and alarm in a paper this morning …
that Miss Nevada will not be able to use her voice during the
season; also the statement that Dr Palmer had two of her
teeth extracted in Salt Lake and was carrying them around
in his pocket exhibiting them to people. I repeat I was
alarmed, because I thought if they were going to take her to
pieces, bit by bit, there would be nothing left of her.

Perhaps this amused her, because five days later, on 23 March,
Nevada sang Amina for him and, four days after that, a highly
successful Mireille.

To counter press reports that he had raked in a hundred and
seventy-five thousand dollars in San Francisco alone, Mapleson
gloomily listed his outgoings:

Madame Patti	$50,000
Railway tickets	$18,400
Other salaries	$80,000 (4 weeks)

That still left a healthy surplus of more than twenty-five thousand dollars, but it illustrates the enormous sums involved –
sums which, by only a small alteration in the margin, could
produce losses as massive as the profits which were ascribed to
him. In Chicago, for example, he took fifty thousand dollars in
advance ticket sales, but meanwhile had spent thirty thousand
on extra scenery for the vast new auditorium (seats for six thousand, with room for another five thousand standing). In all, a
hundred and ninety thousand people were estimated to have
attended the opera that fortnight. To fund a weekly turnover of
the equivalent of about one and a half million pounds at today's
prices, Mapleson must have had very substantial arrangements
with the banks, and at any one time he might be considerably
either in credit or in deficit, since box-office income and salary
payments would not exactly correspond.

Returning to London by way of an extended excursion to Chicago and then back to New York again, Mapleson claimed to have brought home a profit on the season of fifty thousand pounds (though Rosenthal suspects that this figure was a product of his habitual exaggeration).

He had certainly (and unexpectedly) had a wonderful winter, and if only he had decided to bank his takings and retire at the age of fifty-five, he would be remembered as the first great impresario to take opera profitably and successfully across the United States. Set against his crushing failure with the abortive Embankment fiasco, this would have provided him with a noteworthy finale, and a comfortable retirement income for himself and his wife (who, a not unusual fate for the wives of Victorian diarists, plays no part in his *Memoirs* at all).

But how could he retire? He had justified the risk. He was living a heady life of achievement and luxury. Queens and Presidents acknowledged his supreme efforts in the cause of High Art. People had mocked, and he had seen them ruined! Of course he must continue.

At the Met., Damrosch had died, to be replaced by Seidl; and at the Academy Augustus Brown had also died, and the stockholders had elected a new President, Herman Le Roy. Mapleson's lease of the Academy had now run out, so he needed to renegotiate there. Meanwhile in London, with the Gyes extinguished he took on the lease of Covent Garden, where he presented a further series of Silver Jubilee performances for Patti, with whom he had agreed a most onerous contract. It stipulated not only that she did not have to rehearse at all, but that she could cancel any afternoon without breaking the contract, leaving Mapleson to bear any loss in ticket sales and the brunt of public discontent. The contract also provided for two thousand pounds to be deposited at Rothschilds' by Mapleson, which was to be forfeited to her in the event of his being unable to provide the total number of shows stipulated. All this, and five hundred pounds a night as well! No wonder he grumbled.

Patti cancelled the first night (*Traviata*), and then the second (*Faust*) too. Mapleson, in desperation, announced that an unknown singer, Mlle Fohlström, would sing Lucia instead, but 'without rehearsal and for her an indulgent reception is craved'. So – still no understudy, and no other soprano kept available either.

It is impossible to believe that Mapleson really cared any more. Certainly he minded the prospect of turning away a theatre full of the paying public, but as to showing enough concern for the integrity of his shows to make the simplest arrangements at minimal cost for rehearsing an understudy from the myriad young singers at his immediate disposal within the company – it seems never to have occurred to him.

As a result, Mapleson's reputation for unreliability continued to grow. Patti's Carmen (unmentioned in the *Memoirs*) was a disaster, but her final night, on 25 July in *Trovatore* and followed by another of his perfunctorily improvised street processions, went well.

Although he had still not negotiated a new lease at the Academy, he proceeded to put a new company under contract for the United States. As he was now without Patti, Scalchi, Nilsson or Nevada, it is not surprising that he advertised it as a 'true ensemble' company. Only when these preparations were complete did he discover that the Academy (whose directors had probably hoped to have seen the last of him, and had spent eighty thousand dollars on redecoration) would agree to let him the building for just three evenings and one matinée a week, and that far from offering him a subsidy they required a substantial rent for this curtailed availability. At other times the Academy was occupied by the new craze – the American Opera, which attracted lavish support for performing in English. Decent performances in English, like first-class performances in German, were *in*, second-rate and under-rehearsed performances from Mapleson's all-too-familiar repertoire were definitely *out*.

With no big names, and no financial backing (which in itself brings ticket sales, from those unwilling to see their money wasted), Mapleson simply put down his head and charged, to utter (and predictable) disaster.

Just as American audiences are exceptionally generous to perceived success, so also they have very little patience with perceived failure. When Mapleson was seen, at his own estimation and by general consent, as the Great Opera Mogul, they were eager to overlook any deficiencies in his shows. But once he had become tarnished, a butt of ridicule even, then those deficiencies were all they saw. Most damning of all, he was no longer *smart*. His public interviews now always contained a mass of complaints, guaranteed to turn people away. Yet that he managed to open at all, when the stage was regularly occupied by other companies, was something of a triumph. His *Carmen*, this time with a specialist, Minnie Hauk, in the title role and with Ravelli and Del Puente (whose voice was described by George Bernard Shaw as 'loose, loud, unsteady and monotonous') supporting her, was a marked improvement on his usual fare of *Sonnambula*-by-numbers – but just as there were few big names on stage, so the big battalions of Old New York were also fading away.

Despite her depressing performance in London, he was pushing Fohlström as his new Gerster in *Lucia*. She cancelled twice through illness, then sang, to rather better reviews than those offered by the London press. But there were many empty seats. Mapleson lowered the prices. People complained that this was letting in the music-hall clientele. His operas – *Lucia*, *Trovatore*, *Carmen*, *L'Africaine*, *La Favorite*, *Faust*, the everlasting *Sonnambula* – were all old-hat to the Academy audience. Had they not seen these same productions, the same costumes even, year on year for the past eight years? And now they could not even brag about seeing and hearing Patti, or Nilsson.

Mapleson produced *Manon*, with Hauk in the title role; as she commented in her autobiography, *Memories of a Singer*, 'only when I threatened to leave did he order rehearsals to begin ... neither was the performance as satisfactory as might have been wished, owing to insufficient rehearsal'. No wonder he had to close the season a fortnight early, humiliated by the decreasing audiences.

He managed to re-engage Lillian Nordica, an American soprano born in Maine, whose sheer grit triumphed over her musical short-comings, once married but now widowed, and this improved his reception in Boston and Philadelphia, where she sang Violetta. But in Chicago a new hazard arose. Hauk prided herself on her realistic acting, but in *Carmen* she grabbed Ravelli, her Don José, with such emotion as he was attempting his high C that the tenor missed his note, and threw so furious a tantrum that the audience burst into applause, captivated by such brilliant acting. Backstage, he went for Hauk; the next morning poor Mapleson was handed a letter from the diva's husband, Baron de Hesse-Wartegg, which began:

> The vile language, the insults, and threats against the life of my wife in the presence of the entire Company, quite incapacitate her from singing further, she being in constant fear of being stabbed ...

This was accompanied by a demand, from her lawyers, for a two thousand dollar bond from Mapleson, as surety that he would protect Hauk from being further harassed. This, very reluctantly, he had to find, if he was not lose her.

Mapleson himself went down again with gout, in Minneapolis, and so despaired of Arditi's health that he prepared a telegram to be sent to the ailing conductor's wife, enquiring what to do with his remains. Both in time recovered, however, and on 20 March they reached San Francisco, having made their customary stops *en route*. In all these towns, however, they met with smaller audiences than they had been used to; yet

the singers' salaries still had to be paid, whether they were performing or not – Patti had certainly exacted huge fees, but these
were only paid if she actually turned up, and her presence guaranteed big houses. Nor did the newspapers help. Mapleson as
an English colonel (however bogus) had lost his novelty value.
Now the best bet for a story was some new example of his mis-
fortune or incompetence.

He opened with his strongest lead, Hauk, in *Carmen*, supported by Ravelli and Del Puente. The *San Francisco Chronicle*
described the troupe as 'dispirited', and intimated that Ravelli
had cut some of his music. On 25 March the company did *Lucia*
with Del Puente taking over as Enrico, the second baritone
having unaccountably refused to appear: the word was that he
had not been paid. Nordica received 'bad news about her
mother', and slipped quietly away. Far more serious were the
small numbers making up the audience: this in itself was an
inhibiting factor for future ticket sales.

Finally, on 10 April, after three weeks of forlorn hopes that
San Francisco would somehow rescue him from disaster,
Mapleson received a writ from Ravelli, demanding four thousand eight hundred dollars, representing two months' unpaid
salary. Others joined him. Ravelli's lawyers impounded all the
company's props and musical scores. On Tuesday 20 April the
company, one hundred and sixty indigent players, were
camping out in the street, having been ejected from their hotels.
The Morning Call described their plight:

> The scene outside the Grand Opera House looked very
> much like Act 3 from *Carmen* – about 100 antique and pic-
> turesque members of Mapleson's chorus and ballet, male
> and female, were sitting or lying on their baggage where they
> had passed the night. As these light-hearted children of
> sunny Italy lay basking in the sun they helped the hours to
> pass by card playing, cigarette smoking, and the exercise of
> other international vices. One could notice that there was a

sort of expectant fear amongst them seldom seen in people of their class.

The word 'antique' must have hurt.

Mapleson was finished. Perhaps nothing became him so well as his conduct to his troupe now, in this bitter retreat. In such situations lesser impresarios, before and since, have been known to simply abandon their people. For all that there was no money, Mapleson continued doggedly to support them. He saw to their hotels, he put up with endless vituperative abuse, he bowed to their strikes, he kept patiently working his way East, dragging with him his grumbling, unhappy, demoralised crew.

In Chicago, where Mapleson stubbornly continued to present his advertised programme (once with just a piano accompaniment, after the orchestra had walked out), there was civil unrest, with bombs, riots and the National Guard patrolling the streets. The company probably did not even notice. Mapleson's belongings were seized again, and released only through the intervention of the unusually generous Fred Peck, President of the Opera Society in Chicago. Among the many pathetic sights to be seen in the city they encountered, as if in a mirror, the similarly stranded members of the Milan Opera Company who, having been their competitors in New York in 1884, had been on the Chicago streets for a fortnight. Mapleson managed to include them in his company's passage back East.

At last they all reached New York. As Mapleson traded his last personal belongings to the International Steamship Office in return for tickets back to Europe for his troupe, one lawsuit at least went his way: he had finally won his case against the United States Customs, who had consistently levied import duty on his (temporarily shipped) costumes and scenery. All the money was repaid to him, plus interest at six per cent.

A creditor warned Mapleson that he had better sail from

New Jersey, since the bailiffs would be waiting for him at New York; but not for the first time the Colonel proved to be one too many for his enemies. He sailed with magnificent insouciance from New York, joining the ship on her way out of the bay, and thus ruined a carefully prepared ambush at New Jersey.

Mapleson landed at Liverpool on 8 June 1886, expecting to find everything ready for a great concert in the Liverpool Exhibition building. But news of his troubles had preceded him, and no one in Liverpool had expected that his company would perform. When they did, few came. The total box-office takings were no more than eighty pounds, of which Mapleson received nothing.

Back in London, Patti, Nicolini, Del Puente and the others generously gave a benefit evening for Mapleson at the Drury Lane Theatre, lent for the night by Augustus Harris. Queen Victoria and the Prince of Wales were named as patrons, and Mapleson received enough from this event to fund a straggling autumn tour round Dublin, Cork, Manchester, Glasgow and Birmingham.

But things had changed in Britain during Mapleson's absence, as they had in the United States. Carl Rosa's new company, performing in English, had become very popular on Mapleson's old route; Rosa even had Mapleson's daughter-in-law Marie Roze as Principal Soprano. Their audiences began to dwindle, until by the time Mapleson and his company reached Bradford, they numbered no more than a hundred.

He carried on, to sour reviews, kept afloat by Patti. Patti now worked for him for a mere six hundred and fifty pounds a night – amazingly, this was by arrangement with Henry Abbey, who had reappeared and signed up exclusive rights to her appearances in London. On 4 June 1887 Mapleson opened in London with *Lucia*, followed by Lilli Lehmann in *Fidelio* and then Patti in *Traviata* ('a good deal was left out', notes Shaw in his *Pall Mall Gazette* review). That night the box-office receipts were a thousand pounds, so he had three hundred and fifty to distribute to the rest of the company, and to meet the rent and all the other costs entailed in the production.

Patti cancelled her next performance, and when Mapleson wrote to remonstrate with her he learnt that she had already left London from Paddington for her castle in Wales.

The British tour limped on through the winter; Mapleson drew on every resource he could think of, in order to keep going on credit until that magic moment when the audiences would flock back to him and the box office would again generate heaps of money with which to pay his debts. Finally, on 27 January 1888, a receiving order was made out against him, and on 24 April he appeared in the Bankruptcy Court. His debts amounted to £42,410, a massive sum when set against his assets of less than five hundred pounds. He was fifty-eight years old, and had no prospects of any kind.

The *Memoirs* were no doubt part of his attempts to make restitution to his many creditors. But after their publication, the shadows close in. He reverted to acting as agent to a few singers based in London, and even managed to cobble together a brief spring season for 1889. Of this, Shaw wrote in *The Star*:

> Mr Mapleson is hammering away again at Her Majesty's with *Il Barbiere, La Sonnambula, Lucia* ... For old times' sake I will let Mr Mapleson's enterprise alone. I know how it must end; how it ended before ... There is something pathetic in Mr Mapleson's conviction that he must be an impresario. There is something cruel in the reply of the world: *Je n'en vois la nécessité.* Alas Mr Mapleson will not learn from me what he refuses to learn from experience.

He spent another seven years in the wilderness, then made a final, and again unsuccessful, reappearance in New York, presenting a short season at the New Academy in the autumn of 1896. Whenever he was asked the cause of his spectacular ruin, he invariably ascribed it, not to his American adventures, but to the failure of the National Opera House on the Embankment.

Mapleson died on 14 November 1901, of Bright's Disease, a degenerative deterioration of the kidneys, at the age of seventy-one. The only mourners at his funeral were a pair of ancient cleaning ladies from Her Majesty's Theatre. He made no Will, as he had nothing to leave. His Obituary in *The Times*, dwelling inaccurately on the comic aspects of his career, brought an angry response from his elder son Henry, then living in Paris:

> That he died a poor man, leaving his widow destitute, and that the many artists and musicians whose fortune he made, have entirely forgotten their indebtedness to him, is sufficiently sad, without having ridicule cast on his memory by *The Times*.

The paper published an apology.

3

Oscar Hammerstein I
(1846–1919)

OSCAR HAMMERSTEIN'S IS the most extreme case of a man who sought money solely in order to present grand opera. In his heyday, he was perhaps the best known man in the United States after the President. Three times he made his fortune, three times he spent it on opera.

A small lonely man, with simple tastes, instantly recognisable from his Napoleon III beard, swallow-tail coat, tall French silk topper and the trade mark cigar clenched between his teeth, he would roam the streets of New York at night, whatever the weather, all alone after some great gala evening had electrified the city's opera-lovers, seeking some respite from the empty glamour of his life. He lived in two rooms in an old theatre, slept in a simple cot, and often went out without even the price of a meal in his pocket. Yet he regularly outbid the Directors of the Metropolitan Opera House in paying the highest fees for opera stars, and his theatres (he built seventeen in all) were famed for their luxurious fittings and lavish gilding.

Oscar Hammerstein was born on 8 May 1846 in Stettin, the son of a Jewish building contractor who shortly afterwards removed with his family to Berlin. His father played the violin and his mother the piano, and he was strictly educated in both instruments and the flute as well, and in all the conventional subjects of his family background.

So far, so normal. But the sudden death of his mother when he was just fourteen had a much more traumatic effect on him even than might be expected from such a sad event. Not only was he deprived of a warm and loving parent; he also lost the one safeguard protecting him from his father, a violent and troubled man who was unable to show affection to his eldest son. It is clear that life at home deteriorated sharply and immediately. Then his father remarried, further increasing the tension within the small household, and when the fifteen-year-old Oscar arrived home late for a Hebrew lesson after an evening's skating, his father beat him so severely that the boy needed stitches in his forehead.

As soon as his father was asleep, Oscar tiptoed out of the house with what little pocket money he had, and his violin, for which a late-night pawnbroker gave him a hundred and sixty-five marks. He bought a third-class ticket to Hamburg that night, and the next morning he boarded a cattle-boat bound for Hull. This passage took four days, but he arrived in time to embark as a steerage passenger on the *Isaac Webb*, a New York-bound freighter. This second voyage cost him a hundred and fifty marks and lasted for eighty-nine days, by which time the migrants, rocked by storms and half-starved in the filthy conditions below decks, were ready to welcome whatever the New World had to offer.

New York in the early months of 1863 was equally ready to welcome anyone willing to work. With most able-bodied men away fighting in the American Civil War, employers were desperate for labour. Within twenty-four hours Hammerstein had found a job at two dollars a week with a cigar-maker named Levine. Here Hammerstein's early training gained him a distinct advantage. Used to long hours, he worked for Levine from seven in the morning until six at night, then cleaned at his boarding-house to pay for his keep, and finally settled down to learn English. There is something heroic in such single-minded persistence in a boy of sixteen, in a foreign country and cut off from all family contact.

Within a month Levine had upped Hammerstein's pay to five dollars a week, and within six months he had moved to smarter lodgings and could afford an occasional night out. This ferocious little dynamo – he was only five foot four inches tall – was already showing a drive and self-discipline that would surely bring him great success.

Hammerstein had first experienced opera as a schoolboy in Berlin, in the course of his studies of composition and musical appreciation, but it was in New York that, in his biographer Vincent Sheean's happy phrase, he sat 'dazed by the splendor, the mysterious but imperative irrationality of opera'. He was eighteen, and this was the 1864 season of the Strakosch Company, a troupe variously led by Maurice Strakosch, Patti's protector, and his brother Max; it included performances of *Faust, Martha* and *Der Freischütz*. From then on, he attended every night he could; he had found the focus of his life, and it was to remain unalterably fixed until his death, fifty-five years later.

Meanwhile, cigars remained his day-job. He made them himself; he supervised others making them; he invented a wooden cigar-mould, but sold it outright to a rival manufacturer for three hundred dollars. A month later he invented a mould that would produce twelve cigars simultaneously, and this time he took out a patent. At the age of twenty he married Rose Blau, the seventeen-year-old sister of a room-mate. They lived in a new apartment on 55th Street beside the East River, by which Hammerstein travelled to and from work by steamboat, and his marriage provided him with his only experience of happy family life: Rose bore him five sons.

In the course of his early excursions to the Strakosch

presentations Hammerstein had become friends with the young composer Adolf Neuendorff, Strakosch's chorus master and subsequently the principal mover in bringing Wagner's works to New York. He and his wife were regular visitors at 55th Street, and the two men constantly discussed how opera could be profitably presented.

As with most businesses, the start-up money is the hardest to find. To hire a theatre, to sign contracts with singers, to engage and rehearse an orchestra, let alone invest in stage scenery and costumes – all this calls for hard cash. But in nineteenth-century New York opera had a bad name among investors, who were more used to hearing of its losses than its profits.

In 1871 Neuendorff, who had previously encouraged Hammerstein in his composing, turned to him for money to invest in an autumn season of opera. With Carl Rosa already a participant in the syndicate, Hammerstein staked his entire savings, five hundred dollars, despite Rose's appalled objections. And so his first season opened on 18 September 1871, with productions including *Martha*, *Der Freischütz*, *Trovatore* and *Lucia di Lammermoor*.

By 15 November the losses had eaten up all their savings. Nevertheless, Hammerstein was ecstatic. He had found his vocation, and from that date until the end of his life, the sole purpose of his many successful business ventures – the manufacture of cigars, his various inventions, property development, newspaper publishing and presenting drama and vaudeville – was to provide stepping-stones to enable him to present opera to as many people and in as many different places as possible.

With these dreams growing within him and with the birth of his second son, Arthur, imminent, Hammerstein sold his multiple cigar mould for fifteen hundred dollars and opened his first bank account. He also became an American citizen – then, as now, a landmark for any immigrant.

Thanks to persistent hard work, his command of the English language had become good enough for him to write both to and for the press, even to attempt a series of short plays. Now he decided to start a trade journal for cigar-makers. Again Rose objected, but this time she was wrong. With a spare fifty dollars he rented a basement for twelve dollars a month, and on 5 May 1874 the first edition of the *United States Tobacco Journal* appeared, with Oscar Hammerstein listed as 'Editor & Publisher'. In fact, he did most of the jobs involved in publishing a journal and getting it out on the streets, including collecting a hundred and twenty dollars from his advertisers on publishing day, and a hundred in subscriptions. By publishing credit lists of retail tobacconists and, later, the market rates in tobacco leaf, the journal rapidly became required reading in the cigar trade, and thus very profitable. How easy life might have been for the Hammersteins, had the architect of their fortunes been content to build on the commanding position he had thus acquired.

About the same time as he launched his journal Hammerstein, now in his mid twenties, also launched into property investment. His first deal, on 116th Street, netted him sixteen hundred dollars in one week and vouchsafed him a dangerously enticing glimpse of Eldorado at the same time. However, Neuendorff was at hand with another scheme, this time to present German culture (revues, music, even a play by O. Hammerstein entitled *Solo Sechzig*) at the renamed 'Germania Theatre' on 14th Street. This venture opened in the autumn of 1874 and ran until the end of 1877, when Neuendorff was recruited to conduct a season of Wagner at the Academy of Music.

Meanwhile, tragedy had struck. Rose Hammerstein died in 1876, soon after giving birth to their fifth son. For the second time, the woman on whose love and support Hammerstein relied entirely was taken from him. It was, in effect, the end for him of domestic happiness. Although he remarried again almost immediately – by arrangement, a suitable girl, Malvina Jacobi, having been found for him by his sister Augusta – the second Mrs Hammerstein, like Mrs Henry Mapleson, remains a shadowy figure, scarcely acknowledged by her husband and apparently tied to a domestic life far from the lurid limelight that illuminated his professional stage-life. The solitary, even ascetic, habits of his later life had their origins in his crushing loss, and opera was to be his only real consolation. Himself a refugee from a tyrannical father, Hammerstein was no softer on his own children, though he maintained his distance more by absence than by violence. His grandson, Oscar Hammerstein II, the famous Broadway composer, records that they were all scared of his grandfather, and yet they loved him too.

Neuendorff's new job as chief conductor at the Academy of Music coincided with the first great Wagner season in New York: *Tannhäuser*, *Lohengrin*, *Der Fliegende Holländer*, and the United States début of *Die Walküre*. Hammerstein was there every night, meeting the cast and entertaining as many as he could afford.

As he was beginning to reinvent himself in a new role, so he chose the traditional stage assistance of a costume: a uniquely high top hat, a tail-coat, a little pointed beard, and a very large cigar. And since, as it transpired, this role was to last a lifetime, the costume became a permanent fixture: the alarming hat remained on, indoors as well as out, the cigar undislodged – even, some thirty years later, when Hammerstein was welcoming the King and Queen of England to one of his performances.

None of this – not the loss of Rose, nor the acquisition of a new persona – was permitted to distract him from the essential business of making money to fund opera, however. He had continued his property speculations in Harlem, highly geared through a complicated series of interlocking mortgages. He was also busy inventing and patenting a pneumatic cigar-making machine, but this he had to sell, for six thousand dollars, when his mortgages threatened to topple.

With hindsight, it seems inevitable that Hammerstein should have fallen victim to the building bug. Obsessive, ambitious, delighting in anything new and adventurous, in love with show and bombast, how could he *not* become involved with building, he who owned so many building sites? He started, modestly enough, with a row of seventeen houses between 7th and 8th Avenues in Harlem. Then, further enriched by cigar royalties, he put up an apartment house on 7th Avenue, between 136th and 137th Street, and named it 'The Kaiser Wilhelm'. It was a typical Hammerstein production – it had a theatre in the basement, and he ran out of money before he could get the roof on – but was finally completed when he took out a further mortgage on his income from the *Tobacco Journal* (which at the time was making him twenty-five thousand dollars a year in profits). After the famous New York blizzard of 1888 he and his sons Harry and Arthur themselves set to work shovelling away the snow which had rudely buried the unfinished building for a month.

The area of New York known as Harlem, a lightly populated area with no more than a few hundred buildings, was still seen at the time as being a long way from the city centre. Hammerstein decided to give Harlem its own theatre, to be designed by himself. So he bought the land, sold the *Tobacco Journal* for fifty thousand dollars, borrowed ten thousand from his new brother-in-law Harry Rosenberg (married to his sister, herself now an immigrant in the wake of her brother) in return for giving him a job in the project, and started digging. Unfortunately there was solid rock beneath the site – the opposite of the problem Mapleson had encountered on the Embankment – and the subsequent struggle to construct the foundations brought him near to bankruptcy. But at last, when he was forty-two, his first theatre was complete – complete, that is to say, as designed by him. It had grand steps, massive arches, gilded mouldings and a generous helping of red plush. But it lacked one usual amenity of such buildings: Hammerstein had omitted to provide for a box office. Nor, despite employing professional architects to oversee the technical drawings, had he satisfied the city's building regulations. This was only the first of many similar struggles he was to be engaged in with bureaucrats apparently unable – or unwilling – to accept the over-riding supremacy of Art over Safety. But – what was most of all to the point – he had christened it: The Harlem Opera House.

On 30 September 1889 the Harlem Opera House opened its doors with a production imported in its entirety from the Lyceum Theater in return for five thousand dollars cash down in advance. Hammerstein was there, of course, in his extraordinary hat, apparently unconcerned by his mounting losses. The next week saw *Little Lord Fauntleroy*, and shortly thereafter an intensive week of Shakespeare, including *Hamlet, Macbeth, The Merchant of Venice* and *Much Ado About Nothing*. Then, on 4 November, the building finally lived up to its name, with seven consecutive per-formances by the Emma Juch Opera Company. Their repertoire was *Faust, Mignon, Carmen, The Bohemian Girl, Maritana, Der Trompeter von Säckingen* and *Der Freischütz*, and the company's eponymous diva sang the roles of Marguerite, Mignon, Carmen and Agathe, with Maria Decca, a hardy survivor from the com-panies of both Colonel Mapleson and Carl Rosa, as Philine.

Hammerstein lost money on all these ventures, but a reverse was never for him the signal for a strategic withdrawal. '*Reculer pour mieux sauter*' was not a phrase in Hammerstein's vocabulary, either now or later in his life, though he might have wryly recog-nised the aptness of its reverse, '*sauter pour mieux reculer*'. Despite the financial failure of Emma Juch and her operas, this was the moment Hammerstein chose to set up his own opera company.

He may indeed have been spurred on in this venture by pique. He had called on E. C. Stanton, the immaculate general director of the (comparatively) new Metropolitan Opera Company, hoping to persuade him to put on a week of per-formances at the Harlem Opera House, only to be rudely shown the door. 'Some people', Stanton is reported to have said, 'think they can come here and take up my time with the most absurd schemes. I should think you would have more sense than to come in here and talk such nonsense to me!'

It is hard to imagine a greater contrast between Stanton, the patrician *intendant* securely shielded from any adverse wind by the Vanderbilt millions on the one hand, and the apparently crazy little mountebank with his ridiculous hat and cigar on the other. Imagine Hercule Poirot calling on Sherlock Holmes: a guaranteed mismatch from the start.

The result was that Hammerstein, enraged, headed straight off to sell his remaining rights in a tobacco patent, for sixty-five thousand dollars. Then he approached the soprano Lilli Lehmann, one of Wagner's original Valkyries and at the time enjoying tremendous acclaim for a recent performance as Norma at the Met. Thanks to his early training, whatever Hammerstein may have lacked in credibility, he more than made up for in genuine musical knowledge and appreciation. Lehmann, who obviously took to him immediately, agreed to a week's engagement presenting *Norma*, *Les Huguenots* and *Il Trovatore*, an intelligently chosen trio, popular and eminently bankable. She also recommended other singers to him, while Hammerstein set himself the enjoyable task of finding second-hand scenery and costumes. He also needed to hire an orchestra, and a chorus.

In opera, as in films, the name of even one great star is enough to open doors and fill seats. Lehmann's name not only brought Hammerstein the co-operation of opera's support industries – costumiers, scenery-works and, crucially, the underworld freemasonry of chorus and musicians – without which the most august impresario might find himself unable to mount a plausible performance; it also brought in the customers, and their money, at two dollars fifty for the best seats, and fifty cents for the cheapest. Every night Hammerstein was there, perched on a kitchen chair in the wings, watching enthralled. And thanks to his own costume – the hat, the tail-coat and the cigar, already in place – he even became part of the spectacle himself.

Hammerstein gained two inestimable advantages from this highly successful week: a good profit, and a reputation as a man who paid his artists promptly. It was the latter, an unusual virtue in his field, that was to help him through innumerable reverses in the future. The history of opera is crammed with unfulfilled promises, of unpresented operas and dishonoured cheques. Hammerstein's name was consistently respected, by those who worked for him, as one whose bearer always kept his word.

The last night, *Trovatore*, on 29 March, ended a triumphant week, and left open the inevitable question: what now? To Hammerstein there would, *could*, be only one answer. Within three days he had acquired a site on 125th Street between 4th and Lexington. On 2 April 1890 he was to be found there, watching men breaking the ground to dig the foundations of a new and larger theatre, only five streets away from his first, named the Columbus.

Despite the opera profits, Hammerstein's first full year at the Harlem Opera House lost fifty thousand dollars, and during the summer of 1890 he sold all his other real estate (thirty houses and twenty-four apartment blocks) to concentrate on his two theatres. On 11 October 1890 both houses were presenting opera: *Roméo et Juliette* at the new Columbus, and *Ernani* at the Harlem. But thereafter, with a unexpectedly sure 'feel' for commercial reality, he promoted a series of highly profitable popular shows at the Columbus – vaudeville, thrillers, even minstrel shows – while concentrating on opera at the Harlem with Neuendorff's wife Georgine von Januschovsky, a soprano, in the leading roles, her husband in the pit, and the remains of the now-disbanded Emma Juch Opera Company of unhappy memory filling in the gaps. Only his production of Ibsen's *The Pillars of Society* – its American première – failed so absolutely that the theatre was dark for a fortnight.

It was this autumn that Mascagni's first opera and only hit, *Cavalleria Rusticana*, was beginning to be talked about as the newest candidate for inclusion on the list of All-Time Great

Operas. Hammerstein was determined to be the man who first presented it in the United States, and paid Mascagni's publisher three thousand dollars, cash down against royalties of fifteen per cent of the gross take, in return for exclusive rights for an American production. This was generous (Debussy's terms for *Pelléas et Mélisande* were a hundred dollars a show). Unfortunately, as Richard D'Oyly Carte had also found, American copyright law was unpredictable. Briefly, the courts seemed to protect an Italian copyright (for example) only if the work had not been given outside Italy. Once performed elsewhere, it was considered to be in the public domain. Hammerstein's rights proved unenforceable, and earlier performances were given in both Philadelphia and Chicago. Worse, Aronson, a rival manager, was known to be preparing a performance in New York with Heinrich Conreid, soon to become *intendant* of the Met., as his stage manager. Conreid was an old enemy of Hammerstein's from the days when, as a successful young actor, he had worked for Hammerstein in 1882 to great acclaim, followed by a very hostile parting.

To be sure of the necessary Press coverage, Hammerstein had decided to present the great première in the fashionable heart of the city, but found that all the suitable theatres were already booked. With no other choice, he took an empty dance hall, the Lennox Lyceum off Madison, and set about converting it into a reasonable approximation of a traditional theatre, constructing a canvas prescenium which in the event failed to impress the critics. A last-minute injunction taken out against Aronson failed, and both performances took place on the same day, 1 October 1891. Aronson, by staging his at the Casino Theater in the afternoon, gained the precedence, but Hammerstein won on musical points: the critics praised his Santuzza (Georgine von Januschovsky), while poking fun at his conversion of the Lyceum.

Incurable optimism and a genius for driving others (especially his sons) as hard as he drove himself may count as two of

Hammerstein's strongest advantages as an impresario, but a generous slice of good luck also played its part. He could never have predicted that his enduring friendship with Neuendorff, no doubt a source of some discord within the Hammerstein household, would provide him access to a soprano of Georgine von Januschovsky's talent and, just as important, stamina: how many friends can be relied upon to marry a woman both able and prepared to sing eleven Santuzzas in twelve days, *and* to critical acclaim?

Not one to accept an affront, as we have seen, Hammerstein determined to fill the gap in his portfolio of theatres (he had already built a second one next door to the Harlem, which he leased to a vaudeville company). With his brother-in-law Harry Rosenberg rewarded with the job of manager at the Harlem, and John Donnelly in charge of the Columbus, he bought a plot on 34th Street between Broadway and 7th Avenue (now occupied by Macy's department store). The Manhattan Opera House, with two thousand six hundred seats, fifty-two boxes and, *mirabile dictu*, a box office too, opened on 14 November 1892 with a season of French plays presented by an independent company. It was, he told assembled journalists, 'one of the handsomest and most modern [theatres] on earth'. He was all the more convinced of this since he had designed it himself, employing the architectural firm of McElfatrick solely to handle the bureaucratic side of the work. (His demands for architectural grandeur were always more exacting than those for rehearsal time.) Its foyer rivalled that of the Palais Garnier in Paris and the Staatsoper in Vienna, and the auditorium was a hundred feet deep.

The problem was, as it turned out, that ordinary theatre played there was inaudible (this was entirely predictable: Hammerstein may have built theatres, but his mind was always on opera houses) and the consequent collapse of the Mayer company which was presenting the French plays produced an unexpected lawsuit. The leading actress, a Mrs Bernard-Beere, sued Hammerstein instead of Mayer. She lost, but the comedy of Hammerstein's appearance in the witness box (both his physical appearance and his gift for repartee) gained him considerable publicity and added to his growing image as a 'character'.

Christmas that year brought the announcement of 'Hammerstein's English Opera Company' at the Manhattan Opera House. The opening repertoire for Spring 1893 included solid shows such as *Carmen, Rigoletto, Fidelio, Il Trovatore*, and *The Bohemian Girl* (readers may be unfamiliar with the great nineteenth-century success of Balfe's opera, which was then considered England's major contribution to the international operatic scene but is now very rarely performed).

The performances seem to have been poorly produced; for example, in *Carmen* half the soldiers had a disconcerting habit of taking aim at the audience instead of the back of the stage. One reviewer, while praising the ubiquitous Mme von Januschovsky, considered that 'the rest of Mr Hammerstein's cast was distinguished chiefly by its unevenness'. The *New York Daily Tribune* described his production of Moszkowski's *Boabdil* as 'unpardonable'. With hindsight, it seems likely that the poor standard of these shows probably owed less to Hammerstein's lack of taste than to his lack of money. Building this monster had taken all his reserves, and its losses exceeded the income from his other theatres. Undismayed, he cheerfully gave press interviews in which he promised to bring up the French opera from New Orleans, and even gave precise cast lists. Nothing happened. The great theatre stayed mainly dark. By July Hammerstein was ready to acknowledge defeat – temporarily. The company was disbanded, and he turned to Koster and Bial, prosperous if down-market promoters of music-hall shows, so successful that they were currently turning paying customers away from their 23rd Street premises.

Hammerstein's proposition, like all the ideas which made him money, was a simple one: the much larger capacity of the

Manhattan Opera House should further increase Koster and Bial's profits, and enable them to employ even more attractive international 'acts': a deal was done. Koster and Bial made their profits principally from the food and drink sold during the shows, so every other row of seats was removed, and tables were fitted. Other additions were a large bar, and a discreet place for clients to entertain favourite artistes. The theatre reopened, renamed 'Koster & Bial's Music Hall', with Hammerstein in charge of booking the performers, his partners of maximising the catering turnover.

Should we be surprised that Hammerstein made a triumphant success of this? After all, it had nothing to do with opera, or cigars, or real estate. What is so impressive about Hammerstein, what no doubt contributed to the love his family felt for him despite the emotional distance he maintained from them, was the enthusiasm with which he threw himself into each new venture. Marie Lloyd, La Belle Otéro, La Carmencita, Cléo de Mérode – the glittering stars of the *Folies-Bergères* and the international cabaret circuit all sailed for New York, drawn by Hammerstein's generous cheques, and drawing, in their turn, New Yorkers in their thousands, who sat happily smoking and drinking while the glamorous Old World artistes performed for fabulous fees. Everyone was happy. What was more, New York itself was booming, and the population – Hammerstein's clientele – was growing at the rate of two hundred thousand a year, every year.

Here then was the second moment when, had Hammerstein, now aged forty-eight, been content to settle for collaborative success without opera, he and his family might have enjoyed peace and prosperity. But there was another facet to his character, already illustrated by his obsessive supervision of the design of his buildings: he *had* to be in control, and this is a characteristic which, while it works well for a sole proprietor, may cause problems in a partnership.

In this case the problem was svelte, petite and came complete with a wiggle. She was called Mademoiselle de Dio, and she had engaged the undivided attention of George Kessler, a champagne salesman much involved with Hammerstein's new partners. Kessler wanted her to sing at the Music Hall, and Koster and Bial were happy to oblige their colleague. No doubt, being human, they took some little pleasure in being able to demonstrate their power to make things happen. Hammerstein did not fall in with this scheme: he refused to book the girl. His partners, having a majority on the board, instructed that she be booked, regardless of his decision.

The delighted Kessler took a number of boxes and packed them with obliging fans of the young *chanteuse*. The curtain rose, the orchestra struck up a tune, Mademoiselle de Dio stepped forward – and Hammerstein, in his own box, stood up and hissed so loudly that the whole audience, well aware that he was the manager of the show, began to laugh. Kessler, aghast, physically attacked Hammerstein in the corridor; the two men were hustled out into the street where they started fighting again, and were promptly arrested. When Koster and Bial were called to the Jefferson Market police station, they bailed out Kessler, but left their partner Hammerstein in his cell.

The whole affair was reported by newspapers all over Europe, much slanted in Hammerstein's favour. A series of lawsuits instituted by him so demoralised his unfortunate partners that to be rid of him they settled out of court, to the tune of three hundred and seventy-five thousand dollars in cash, plus a mortgage of three hundred thousand on the theatre.

Time to buy a pension? 'I will build', proclaimed Hammerstein, 'a house the like of which has never been seen in the *whole world*.' Within two years, the success of this new theatre had ruined Kloster and Bial; within three years, Hammerstein himself was broke.

The site for the new venture, the Olympia, was found by the demolition of a disused armory on Broadway and two adjacent houses on 44th and 45th Streets. The whole measured a massive two hundred and three feet by a hundred and fifty-four, and on 14 March 1895 Hammerstein announced that it would contain no fewer than four theatres, interconnected, with joint services, and all to open on 15 November. There was to be the Olympia Music Hall, seating two thousand eight hundred; the Concert Hall; the Lyric Theater; and finally the Roof Garden, which would also be available for staging entertainments. On top of this, there would be bars, a restaurant, a billiard room, even an Oriental café, and all designed by Hammerstein himself, with the long-suffering McElfatricks struggling in his wake to get the multiplying plans passed by the sceptical city building regulators.

With a work-force of a thousand labourers, the Olympia opened only ten days late. Hammerstein's second son, Arthur, now aged twenty-three, was actively engaged in the decorating, and the theatre featured Hammerstein's own patented system of air-conditioning. The paint was still wet, but the whole complex seated six thousand, Hammerstein had sold ten thousand tickets at fifty cents each, and the police struggled all night to maintain order. He took out a mortgage of nine hundred and sixty thousand dollars on the completed building, and reserved one small room in it for himself: it contained a piano, and a plain little cot. Public magnificence and private simplicity: these had come to exemplify the Hammerstein way of life.

His first star, the French *diseuse* Yvette Guilbert, was paid a massive four thousand dollars a week (she was able to command an equivalent level of fee in St Petersburg), but thanks to her world-wide popularity he was taking fifteen thousand. However, Hammerstein had a rather unfortunate habit of deliberately engineering quarrels with his stars, when it suited him, as a means of inducing them to cancel their contracts. He seems to have done so less from a desire to avoid paying their fees than from either resentment at their success, or a distaste for the high-handedness which sometimes follows in its wake.

Whatever its cause, it was essentially self-defeating. As soon as Guilbert left, Hammerstein's takings slumped, to four thousand dollars a week – the usual story. He replaced her with the Tiller Girls (from England), then the Cherry Sisters (from Nebraska) – an act so comically awful that audiences were actually encouraged by Hammerstein's sons to throw vegetables, the women on stage being protected by a special net. This was followed by 'Operatic Tableaux', which seem to have been little more than an excuse to display some scantily-dressed sopranos, and thus set off a highly satisfactory (because widely publicised) scandal.

But money continued to pour out rather than in, and worse was to follow. Not only did Hammerstein revive his attempts to compose (he tried his hand at an opera, *Santa Maria*, a ballet, *Marguerite*, and two musical comedies, all equally unsuccessful), but he fell in love with the first of a long series of plump young women with pretty voices, in this case Alice Rose. Engineering a quarrel with the current lead of a French musical, *La Poupée*, he rewarded Alice Rose with the part. Audiences dwindled away, and when Arthur Hammerstein rashly suggested bringing back the Cherry Sisters' net, his father threw an ashtray at him. On 8 June 1898, after a disastrous run of Hammerstein's own musical *War Bubbles*, the Olympia closed.

The New York Life Insurance Company held the mortgage, and when John McCall, the president, wrote to suggest that one of the company's own accountants be brought in to help run the theatre, Hammerstein wrote back in his own hand:

I am in receipt of your letter, which is now before me, and in a few minutes it will be behind me.

Respectfully yours,
Oscar Hammerstein

McCall, not unnaturally, promptly foreclosed, and on 29 June the Olympia was sold at auction, making several thousands more than its book value. Hammerstein was, however, literally penniless. His son Arthur gave him five hundred dollars out of his savings of seven hundred, but this too went on settling other small outstanding debts. As always, Hammerstein's artistes and employees had all been properly paid off. Knowing that he had four hundred dollars hidden in his cot in the Olympia (from which he had been barred by a Court Order) he sneaked up the fire-escape to retrieve the money, was caught, arrested and brought before the judge on a charge of Contempt of Court.

> I have (he told the Court) lost over one million dollars in my efforts to entertain the New York public. Thirty-six years of labor have gone for nought. A stranger is in possession of all its fruits. Your Honor, you can hardly realize the tension under which a music-hall manager such as I have been must do his work. He has to plunge into enterprises with every fiber of his brain on the alert. Through years of unremitting labor I had acquired one million dollars. I put it into a great amusement palace. Now a strange being has the right to say to me: 'Get out! If you dare to touch a pin in this building I will have you arrested!' He has taken possession of my thirty-six years of labor.

Notwithstanding the shaky nature of this reasoning, the judge ordered the four hundred dollars to be handed over to Hammerstein, and dismissed the charge of contempt. Certainly no one could quarrel with his claim of unremitting labour. How Koster must have relished the downfall of his enemy, and how he must have regretted that Bial, who had died exhausted shortly after their epic lawsuit, had not lived to see it.

It was at this time, at the age of fifty and bankrupt, that Hammerstein, magnificently undismayed, spotted the 'finest site in New York for a theater', on the corner of 7th Avenue and 42nd Street. The property, divided among a number of heirs, was being handled by an administrator, and Hammerstein sought him out in order to do a deal. Faced with his strange-looking visitor, now notoriously broke and widely known as a 'cantankerous crackpot', this man must have had nerves of steel to grant him a twenty-year lease with an option to extend, at a rent of eighteen thousand dollars a year, and no deposit required.

But Hammerstein did again what he had done so successfully in the past – he invented and patented something, this time a device for adjusting men's linen sock-suspenders, which he sold for three hundred dollars. Next he produced a machine for recycling tobacco stems, which previously had been discarded as waste. This he sold for twenty-five thousand dollars, which he immediately converted into a team of builders complete with all the necessary materials to build a theatre. Determined to open, as he had announced with his usual bravado, by 2 March 1899, he ran out of money before the roof could be completed – not the first time this had happened. He was already over-borrowed again, and the main contractor refused to continue without a payment of two thousand dollars on account. Travelling, as he always did, in a trolley car one day he found himself next to a young woman who had been employed by him in the chorus line of *Santa Maria*. Recognising him, she took the opportunity to thank him for his past kindness. This was a big mistake: by the end of the conversation she had taken him to her bank and made him a loan of the two thousand, in cash. The moral behind this lifeline so unexpectedly thrown him is to be found in Hammerstein's basic integrity. Utterly irresponsible with his own and with corporate money, he yet had always looked after his individual employees carefully. And on this occasion, as it would again, previous virtue gained him present financial reward.

Deliberately modelled on Paris's *Folies-Bergères*, the Victoria opened (just) on 2 March, as Hammerstein had announced. The red plush cost fifty dollars in a fire-loss sale, and the carpets, at twenty-five cents a yard, came from a superannuated ocean liner. The décor was white and gold, because the 'white' was unpainted plaster. Light-bulbs were recessed into the cornices, to conceal the absence of proper fittings. But the public loved it, and they loved Hammerstein. He had become a national icon, the apparently irrepressible immigrant, the little man in the funny hat who just bounced back however hard you hit him. His bravado was justified, his insane optimism was constantly being fulfilled. Best of all, instead of resorting to the begging bowl, he constantly drew from his own inner resources on an inexhaustible fund of apparently dotty designs and inventions that made real money. His appearance, on his kitchen chair beside the stage, engendered more applause than the acts he hired.

There was no stopping Hammerstein. He built another theatre the following year, the Republic, next to the Victoria, which also gave him the opportunity to build a large roof garden, the Paradise, extending over both buildings and designed for presenting operetta. It included a 'Swiss Farm' complete with a cow, two ducks, a goat, and a monkey specially trained to reach up under the ladies' skirts. By contrast, he was also presenting a dramatisation of Tolstoy's *Resurrection*, which ran for eighteen months and netted him a hundred thousand dollars in profit.

Learning from his experience with Koster and Bial, he now began to place far more emphasis on catering, having recognised its capacity for generating greater profits. In 1904 he revamped the Victoria and it was soon producing four thousand dollars a week net profit – and this in an age still unfamiliar with the stringent demands of income tax. Clearly, opera was about to return to the agenda.

Among Hammerstein's most important assets were his sons, and he was fortunate to be able to draw both on their talents, and on their love for him. Arthur was now a building contractor in his own right with a well-developed appreciation of operetta, whereas Willie's skills lay in an apparently morose (on his part) but meticulous presentation of vaudeville and the Music Hall. Both might be excused for hating grand opera.

The Victoria was acquiring a reputation for presenting 'sensations', acts performed by people who had acquired an overnight notoriety, for example a woman who had unexpectedly been acquitted of murdering her husband. One man even offered to commit suicide on stage. Hammerstein turned him down, enquiring what he would do for an encore. Barnum's circus performers, the young Charlie Chaplin, Buster Keaton, Don the Talking Dog – the Victoria offered an unending stream of entertainment that ran daily from 1.45 in the afternoon until six, and then again from 7.45 in the evening until midnight.

Hammerstein, supported and encouraged by Willie, tried everything: snake-charmers, 'Sober Sue', a young black woman paid twenty dollars a week from whom it was claimed that no one could provoke a smile (her face was paralysed) – a challenge that brought all the leading comedians onto their stage *for free*! There was even a performing bear, which ran amok one evening and which Hammerstein himself subdued. It all made good copy for the newspapers, and it was all massively successful.

In 1905 an extra appearance was widely advertised: 'The One, the Only, the Original Oscar Hammerstein – Début Extraordinary.' Vincent Sheean reports that he 'came out to tremendous applause, sang a song, made a few jokes, and recited a monologue. There was a fifteen-minute demonstration afterward and it was difficult for the rest of the show to proceed.' One can imagine.

Like Mapleson's Duke in *Rigoletto* and John Christie's Beckmesser, the performance was not repeated: sufficient for the impresario to give employment to the trained artiste. Yet one cannot altogether escape the feeling that, *au fond*, an urge to perform may sometimes lurk behind the urge to present. Unacknowledged, perhaps even guiltily concealed, such a yearning may be quickly assuaged by the cruel reality of actually facing a live audience. But certainly in Hammerstein's personal appearance, as also in Mapleson's, there were always clear signs of a deliberate (and perhaps professionally justified) exhibitionism.

Now aged fifty-six, Hammerstein bought a plot on 34th Street, west of 8th Avenue. Here he started to put up what he publicised as a building, to be called the Drury Lane Theater, designed to present the 'greatest spectacles yet seen' – but which everyone, especially his long-suffering sons, tacitly assumed would be for grand opera. At the same time, freed from fiscal restraint by the handsome profits from the Victoria, he was simultaneously building another, smaller theatre, the Lew M. Fields on 42nd Street, named for its eponymous tenant. In this building, his eighth, he installed his latest invention, a gridiron built into the roof that carried two five-thousand-gallon tanks of water, as a precaution against fire, an ever present threat in wooden buildings lit by gas.

Naturally, all this activity placed a great strain on him, both physically and mentally. He collapsed in the street, and spent the next four weeks in hospital. When he was discharged, he was ordered to rest. Indignantly he protested: 'I lead a life of great simplicity. I eat little and drink nothing and smoke only twenty-five cigars a day.'

The time for subterfuge was now past. The Drury Lane Theater's mask was torn aside, and it was triumphantly re-christened The Manhattan Opera House. The outer shell continued to rise, and Arthur was summoned by Hammerstein and asked to abandon his own business in order to work full-time with his father. Willie was, as usual, to produce the money at the Victoria while Arthur, with his father, was to spend it at the Manhattan.

The *Encyclopaedia of New York City* (1995), incidentally, notes that 'Hammerstein designed all his theater buildings, which were praised for their impressive interiors and acoustics. None survive.' They are wrong. At 311 West 34th Street, the Manhattan Center, owned by the Unification Church, is

Hammerstein's second Manhattan Opera House, sadly modified but still there.

As he had with his other theatres, and thanks no doubt to his relentless early training in music, Hammerstein took immense trouble over the acoustics. For example, on his father's instructions Arthur laid the hardwood floor of the orchestra pit over an eighteen-inch-deep layer of broken glass, evidence that Hammerstein would consider anything if he thought it would help him gain his goal. An elliptical sounding board was suspended above the pit in the form of a hung ceiling edged with a hollow plaster beam. The body of the theatre itself was broad enough to allow the audience a close view – a marked contrast, for example, to the long, deep structure of the Metropolitan Opera House. The Met. had been the undisputed centre of opera in New York since the demise of the old Academy, the latter's summary ejection of Colonel Mapleson having proved the most perfect Pyrrhic victory in the sense that no other tenant ever presented opera there again. The Academy's old-money stockholders, so indignant against the Colonel's gallant efforts on their behalf, were reduced to joining the queue for the second-best boxes at the Met., where parterre boxes were now changing hands privately for more than a hundred thousand dollars – say, three million pounds at 1998 values.

While Arthur built the theatre, with its three thousand-odd seats, his father was busy assembling the company. This time he faced an additional problem. At long last the Met. had come to take Hammerstein seriously, and menacing noises began to circulate about the uncertain employment prospects of anyone accepting work with him. But again his good relations with former employees paid off. This time it was Bianca Lescout, originally in his Manhattan Opera production of *The Talisman*, now a distinguished and influential member of the Italian musical establishment, who arranged the appropriate introductions for him to circumvent the Met.'s attempted embargo. As always, however, his greatest ally was his own ability to persuade.

At that time the most famous soprano in the world was Nellie Melba, an imperious, hard-headed battle-axe of a woman. Built like a tank, she confounded every stereotype of a prima donna. Helen Porter Mitchell, daughter of an Australian Presbyterian builder, sometime wife of a Queensland farmer and mother of his son, she suddenly upped and left farm, husband and child and sailed to England on the modest inducement of an offer from Sir Arthur Sullivan of a possible job in the chorus of the D'Oyly Carte troupe. Stopping off in Paris, she had an introduction to Etelka Gerster's singing teacher Mathilde Marchesi who, recognising her immense talent, spent the next six years teaching her technique. From then on her career spiralled upwards in a dizzying series of glamorous gala successes, starting in Brussels and taking in Vienna, London, Paris, St Petersburg, and all this was accompanied by an intense (and intensely fashionable) *affaire* with the young Bourbon Pretender, the Duc d'Orléans.

With Melba's background of glitz and brouhaha, it was no wonder Hammerstein felt he had to travel to Paris himself, to Garnier's richly ornate Grand Hotel on the boulevard des Capucines, to recruit her, an expedition which was no light matter in a lumbering Atlantic steamer.

In her autobiography, *Melodies & Memories*, Melba devotes no fewer than ten pages to the various attempts Hammerstein made in his recruitment drive. At first she refused to see him at all, certain that he wanted her to sing in New York and equally certain that she had no intention of going there. Hammerstein, undeterred, persuaded Melba's old friend from the Palais Garnier, Maurice Grau, to write begging her as a personal favour to him to see Hammerstein. Reluctantly she agreed to do so.

She describes her visitor as 'a determined man of Jewish persuasion, shortish, thin and dark, with piercing black eyes. He carried a top hat with a very wide brim in his hand, and he addressed me in a strong American accent.' Although Melba presents large sections of her memoirs in the form of conversation, this was the only occasion she dignified with a full-scale dramatisation.

Myself: I have no intention of going to New York.

Hammerstein: I shall give you $1500 a night.

Myself: Please don't discuss terms, Mr Hammerstein, because I assure you that is useless.

Hammerstein: It'll be the biggest thing you have done yet. Oscar Hammerstein says so!

Myself: And Nellie Melba says 'No'. I have no intention of going. Good morning, Mr Hammerstein.

Never one to give up easily, Hammerstein settled in to besiege his chosen prey, bombarding her with weekly visits, notes, and telephone calls, even on one occasion getting into her rooms while she was in the bath, and hammering on the bathroom door:

Hammerstein (shouting through the keyhole):
              Are you coming to America?

Myself (between splashes):
              No!

Hammerstein: I'll give you two thousand five hundred a night.

Myself: Not for ten times the money.

Hammerstein: And you can sing as many nights as you like.

Myself: Go away!

Not even this deflected him from his purpose. A few days later, he burst into her room while she was quietly reading a newspaper and announced that he could give her three thousand dollars a night – this at a time when the Met. chorus was paid fifteen dollars a week, or three dollars per show.

Despite Melba's protests he proceeded to scatter thousand-franc notes all over the floor. When she collected them up after he had gone, she found he had left a hundred thousand francs, the equivalent of twenty thousand dollars (or three hundred thousand pounds at 1998 values) and more than ten per cent of the French State's annual subsidy to the Paris Opera.

Hammerstein had not miscalculated. Money was more important to Melba even than it was to most divas, not least because of her own extravagances. Although she took the money to Rothschilds' and instructed them to hold it for Hammerstein to collect, the battle was won: she embarked for New York, arriving at the beginning of December.

By this time, the 1906 winter opera season was fast approaching and Hammerstein had a strong team under contract: the tenors Alessandro Bonci, Amadeo Bassi and Charles Dalmorès; the baritones Mario Ancona and Maurice Renaud; the sopranos Emma Calvé and now Melba; a chorus selected with unusual care; and all presided over by his most crucial appointment, the Italian conductor Cleofonte Campanini. Hammerstein originally tried to recruit Arturo Toscanini, but found him no more amenable to persuasion than did Conreid, who was trying to get him for the Met. Toscanini, a force in opera since his electrifying metamorphosis from second 'cello to conductor at the age of nineteen during a performance of *Aïda* in Rio de Janeiro, was labouring single-handedly and with an obstinacy that was beginning to bring success to stamp out all the abuses (long tolerated by managers like Mapleson) that had disgraced opera with so many second-rate performances – non-compulsory rehearsals, inadequate orchestras, endless encores of the 'lollipop' tunes. He even managed to persuade women in the audience to remove their hats. In short, Toscanini was a man of Hammerstein's stamp.

Failing with Toscanini, Hammerstein imported one of the new breed of stage directors from Brussels, and surrounded himself with a strong administrative and back-stage team, with Arthur as his principal aide. All New York saw this enterprise as a direct challenge to the 'Met.' – the heavy-weight of Broadway, currently directed by his old enemy Heinrich Conreid, who was now a rich man with a hundred and fifty thousand dollars' worth of stock in the Met. management company (a half-share) and was drawing a salary of twenty thousand a year on top of this. Moreover, the Met. had grown used to basking in its social and musical predominance in the world of grand opera.

It was not even as though Hammerstein made any effort to co-operate. The Met. performed each week on Monday, Wednesday, and Friday, and then gave two shows on Saturday. Insisting that he 'needed' to keep Tuesdays and Thursdays for rehearsals, Hammerstein announced that his performances would exactly match the Met.'s. Not only that, he would also be presenting a similar repertoire and, he announced, 'in every respect the superiority of the Manhattan Grand Opera Company to the already existing grand opera is readily apparent'.

There was to be a chorus of a hundred, an orchestra of seventy-five; the Stage Manager was the familiar figure of Charles Wilson (an old Mapleson hand); and the subscription price for a box for the eighty shows planned was four thousand dollars. Orchestra stalls were three dollars, the Dress Circle two dollars fifty, and the cheapest tickets a dollar. (Equivalent seats at the Met. were priced slightly higher, from five dollars down to a dollar.) One detail Hammerstein was careful *not* to publicise was that so far he had only banked thirty thousand dollars in advance box-office sales.

It was rather as though what he really needed was the pressure of possible failure. For all the superb quality of his principal stars, he had no comparable second string, no quality artistes to fall back on in the (far from unusual) event of someone becoming ill. And now, instead of choosing days when the whole of the New York opera audience was available to buy his tickets, he picked those when the strongly-established rival company was already offering similar works. What was it with this old man? Here he was, sixty years of age, with children and grandchildren to consider, staking huge sums which he had made himself in utterly unnecessary risks.

Billy Guard, Hammerstein's press agent, kept up a steady stream of teasing stories of the 'Hammerstein's Lost Tenor ... last heard of in Buenos Aires ...' type. But Bonci had disembarked in good time, on 18 November, and the others were on their way.

Meanwhile, the Met. opened for the season on 26 November 1906. Six blocks away, on 34th Street, Campanini was struggling to rehearse his orchestra above the crashings and hammerings of Arthur's frantic last-minute attempts to complete the Manhattan. He was running late, and his father had to announce a delayed opening, on Monday 3 December. The only light relief was that Caruso, the Met.'s principal prop, had just been arrested in the monkey-house of the Central Park Zoo for molesting Hannah Stanhope, an impressionable young woman. *Artistes*! No one minded (except Conreid, who had a nervous breakdown). An immigrant stevedore might have been deported, but Caruso ... The applause for him that night was as loud as ever.

On 3 December the sun shone between fitful squalls of rain. 'Last Workmen to leave New Manhattan as arrival of audience begins' read that day's (accurate) headline of the *New York American*. The opera to be given was Bellini's *I Puritani*, and every one of the three thousand one hundred seats had been sold. The standing room was crammed, there were massed crowds outside, perhaps just to see the legendary 'crackpot' Hammerstein, with his funny hat and his large cigar, and New York's latest celebrity, Alessandro Bonci, aged thirty-six to Caruso's mature fifty-two.

The rivalry between Bonci and Caruso (like that once

1. James Henry Mapleson

2. The National Opera House (south elevation)

3. Mapleson's chief rival, Frederick Gye

4. Adelina Patti

5. The New York Academy of Music

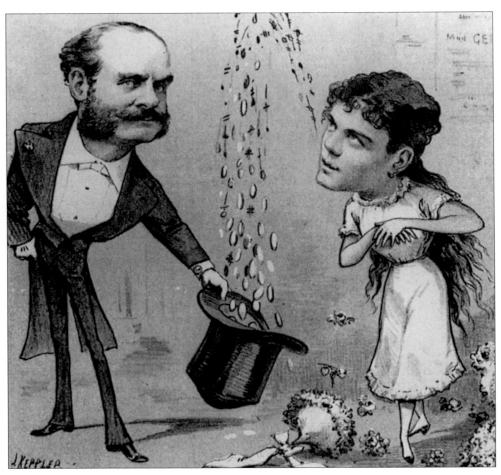

6. Cartoon of Mapleson with Etelka Gerster

7. Oscar Hammerstein I

8. Dame Nellie Melba

9. Mrs Astor

10. Mary Garden

11. Lina Cavalieri
(*left*) and Alessandro
Bonci

12. Hammerstein with the Manhattan Opera House plans

13. The Manhattan Opera House

14. The New York Metropolitan Opera House

15. Enrico Caruso

16. Otto Kahn

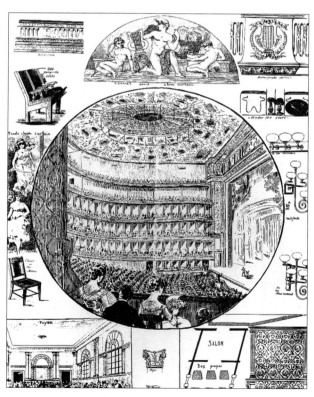

17. The interior of the Met.

18. John Christie at the wheel

19. Three generations: Augustus, William and John Christie

20. Glyndebourne as originally extended by John Christie: the house on the left, the organ room in the centre and the opera house on the right

21. Audrey Mildmay

22. John and Audrey Christie with their children Rosamond and George

23. The 1934 Glyndebourne Company; Fritz Busch (*centre*) with
Audrey Mildmay and Ina Souez beside him

24. Audrey Mildmay as Susanna and John Brownlee as Count Almaviva
in the 1934 production of *Le Nozze di Figaro*

25. Fritz Busch, John Christie and Carl Ebert in the garden at Glyndebourne

26. The Glyndebourne audience

reported between Domingo and Pavarotti) has been much exaggerated, perhaps even encouraged by the protagonists for publicity purposes (there were of course persistent rumours of an imminent duel).

Caruso, on something short of fifteen hundred dollars per performance for sixty-two shows that season, had in any case long abandoned singing Arturo in *Puritani*. His was a more robust instrument, with its world-famous ringing top C, whereas Bonci excelled in a more subtle style and musicality. But the crowds loved the 'details' of their 'feud', and always hoped for more.

But all was not well backstage. Campanini had decided to quit unless a different concert-master was brought in, and first the carpenters and then the chorus threatened to strike. Hammerstein dealt with these last-minute horrors by gracefully giving everyone what they wanted. Even so, he must have been mightily relieved when Campanini took up his baton, half an hour late at eight-thirty, to conduct the inaugural National Anthem, and even more so three hours later when the final curtain came down and he was able to walk out in front of the footlights and address the enthusiastic audience (which included Otto Kahn, a Director of the Met.):

I have no board of directors, nobody to tell me what I should and should not do [laughter]. The ensemble which surrounds this institution is so large and is composed of so many celebrities of music that every opera for the next 3 or 4 weeks is experimental, and depends for success on this audience and this city [applause and cheers].

It may be that it even added to the fun when some members of the audience discovered later, from the state of their clothes, that the paint on the walls had not yet dried.

*

To the distress of some and to the added pleasure of others, there has always been a social element to the presentation of grand opera. This might be endemic (in a clear descent from that first-ever night in Florence, where the audience were an invited group) but was sometimes deliberate (as in the Academy's and subsequently the Met.'s control over who might, or might not, take one of their boxes – the so-called 'Diamond Triangle'). But whether it is seen as good or bad, the social aspect has a definite marketing potential, one which vulnerable impresarios ignore at their peril. Few impresarios have been as vulnerable as Hammerstein, but none has ever turned his back on 'society' with such rugged determination.

Was this because he associated old New York 'society' with the Met., the organisation whose *intendant* had so rudely rejected him sixteen years earlier? If so, he was making the commonplace error of taking people at their own estimation; *old* New York (the Astors and the Prices) still looked on the Vanderbilts and the Kahns of the Met. as irredeemably *arriviste*.

Meanwhile, the line he took was working. Even when his third night (*Faust*) was a box-office flop because Dalmorès was insufficiently big a 'name', the critics loudly praised his conductor, his chorus and his orchestra. He took eleven thousand dollars at the box office the first night, but only ten thousand in total for the next six nights.

As if that first week were not enough, he charged into the second with *Rigoletto, Don Giovanni* and *Carmen*. What must the rehearsal schedule have been like? Six first nights in ten days, with first-class casts: this was opera promotion on a magnificent, not to say prodigal, scale, especially as his subscription (as distinct from box-office) receipts had in the end amounted to less than fifty-three thousand dollars. Hammerstein's feat was perhaps only matched by Thomas Beecham, who at his own personal expense (without regard to profitability) promoted an extravagant London programme at His Majesty's and Drury Lane, and he had inherited his money (a frequent precursor to prodigality), whereas Hammerstein had amassed his fortune by his own hard work and ingenuity. Successful tycoons since the days of Maecenas have often transmuted their gains massively into architecture, resulting in the great palaces of Europe and the Americas. Here was a man whose 're-investment' brought together opera casts rather than house-parties, built theatres rather than mansions.

It is a measure of how opera life had changed since Mozart's day that when Hammerstein asked his leading mezzo, Clotilde Bressler-Gianola, to sing on two consecutive evenings (because there was no one else to do it), her immediate response was that she had 'never *heard* of such a thing'; yet when *Die Zauberflöte* opened at Vienna's Theater auf der Wieden on 30 September 1791, with a cast that included a twenty-three year old Sarastro (Franz Xaver Gerl), it ran seven nights a week with the same cast. Ninety years later (and admittedly with a vast expansion in the sheer volume of space devoted to opera, within which the singers were expected to make themselves heard), a much less strenuous regime was expected, illustrating a shift of influence away from the composer and towards the individual singer which was also reflected in their relative rewards.

Nevertheless, Bressler-Gianola's Carmen proved immensely successful. Played for sex rather than for glamour, it stunned audiences long used to a more reserved (not to say static) style of delivery. Hers, reported *The New York Sun*, was 'an elemental, utterly frank, physical Carmen'. No wonder she delivered for her employer the agreeable financial rewards that flow from packed houses.

Subsequent weeks brought productions of *Trovatore*, *Aïda* and *Lucia di Lammermoor*, and then, just before Christmas, Melba arrived. The *apparatchiks* of the Met. must have been groaning in despair, and one can imagine the state of mind of their pay-masters, the Vanderbilts and the Kahns, who were spending so much money, and to so little acclaim; not to mention that of Caruso, whose participation in an Italianised version of

Meyerbeer's *L'Africaine* was not enough to prevent its immediate demise. Hammerstein was at his zenith.

Melba, under contract to give ten performances, opened on Wednesday 2 January as *La Traviata*, when it was rumoured that she would be wearing two and a half million dollars' worth of jewellery, including one of Marie Antoinette's necklaces (no doubt an heirloom belonging to her Royal lover). What is more, she had initiated a practice whose exhaustive development in the latter part of the twentieth century she could hardly have foreseen: she had recently been insisting on updating the action of *Traviata*, an opera normally performed in seventeenth-century dress, to the period when it was written: 1848.

Delighting in her role as Hammerstein's guardian angel and fêted as the world's greatest soprano, Melba sang fifteen performances, sometimes twice a week, and her Gilda in a performance of *Rigoletto* with Bonci as the Duke and Renaud in the title role, all under the fiercely disciplined baton of Campanini, was described by the *New York Times* as 'the best production seen in New York for many years'.

Not that she had lost any of her famous temperament. In a newspaper interview, Hammerstein was asked the most pertinent question of all by Walter Pritchard Eaton: why he had chosen to be an opera impresario rather than a cigar czar?

He smiled and his eyes squinted as they do when he doesn't wish you to know whether he's ironic or not, and he said, 'Ah, but the tobacco business is prose, this is poetry – you know? It's more fun to make Melba sing than it is to make a cigar. Tonight, now: first she tells me it's too hot in her dressing-room; then it's too cold ...'

And so on. He obviously adored every minute of it.

The Met., whose own much-trumpeted première of *Salome* had to be curtailed because of complaints about its immorality, continued to fight back. Their first (subterranean) manoeuvre had been to instigate an attempt by the Ricordis, Puccini's publishers, to prevent Hammerstein (and Melba) from presenting *La Bohème*. This took the form of a two-pronged attack – first a letter (five months beforehand), followed by a court application in October for an injunction against Hammerstein; and second, the threat of banning his conductor, Campanini, from working in those Italian opera houses where the Met.'s influence was, understandably, sufficiently strong to enforce such control. As an extra, third, precaution, the Ricordis identified (and had numbered) all those (few) orchestral scores already issued, and did what they could to ensure that they would not become available to Hammerstein. What made this effort especially absurd, and particularly distasteful to the public, was that countless performances had already been given, for which the Ricordis had happily accepted a hundred and fifty dollars a night in royalties.

Never one to shirk a fight, Hammerstein managed to delay the proceedings for issuing the injunction, which gave him time to comb Europe for a score – in vain: the Ricordis' instructions were not such as would be lightly ignored. But at last a rather crumpled and incomplete version was obtained. Campanini had no intention of risking being barred from working in his homeland by publicly conducting the work, but he knew the piece almost by heart, and so was able to prepare the missing parts and guide the orchestra through the piece. Puccini, who was himself in New York for the Met.'s première of his *Madama Butterfly*, refused to be drawn into the squabble, perhaps indicating the general distaste for the tactics employed by the Ricordis – and, by inference, the Met.

On 1 March, with the injunction proceedings still pending, Hammerstein's *La Bohème* opened with Melba as Mimi and Campanini sitting innocently in a box, coolly watching his orchestra being conducted by his colleague Fernando Tanara, for all the world as though he himself had had nothing to do with it. As soon as the three performances had been completed,

Hammerstein stopped contesting the injunction, which was promptly granted against him – but too late.

Yet this was a small victory compared to his success in contriving to replace the departing Melba with her almost equally famous rival, Emma Calvé, a French soprano who combined magnificent disciplined singing with the most intense and carefully thought-through acting style, copied from the Italian dramatic actress Eleanora Duse. All in all, she was a very worthy replacement. Not only that, he even managed to persuade both divas to dine with him, on stage, after Melba's final show on 25 March: a *Bohème* which, for good measure, she followed first with the Mad Scene from *Lucia*. Then, after twenty-three curtain calls and a forty-minute standing ovation, a piano was wheeled on to the stage, and Melba accompanied herself in the song 'Mattinata'.

Anxious to be certain of his next season, Hammerstein had also managed to borrow four hundred thousand dollars, secured on the opera house, from Frank Woolworth, who also took a box for every performance.

This night, Melba's last, was Hammerstein's finest hour. With the money for his next season safely secured there he sat, the two great divas one on either side of him, at a dinner which included *suprême de volaille Hammerstein* and *pêche Melba*. To crown it all, the orchestra was playing a medley he had composed himself, entitled 'Memories of the Manhattan Opera Season'. He had achieved more, surely, than he could ever have hoped – presenting indisputably top-class opera in the cultural heart of his adopted country, financially secure, world-famous, enjoying the love and respect of his family as well as substantial wealth through his own efforts – and, perhaps best of all, providing considerable and very public discomfort for his enemies at the Met. who had presumed to mock him. What would not the world's favourites give to be forewarned of the turning-point in their ascent, the more to appreciate their time in the sun? Hammerstein's career had reached its apex. Though there were still some triumphs to come, the shadows were lengthening backstage.

Melba, embarking for France, issued a statement to the press:

I have never enjoyed any season in America so much as the one now closing. All through I have been in splendid health and spirits and I shall never forget the kindness with which I have been received. I am proud to have been associated with Mr Hammerstein in his launching of New York's new opera house. What courage Mr Hammerstein has shown and what wonders he has done! I think there must be something in the conditions of American life to encourage him, for I know of no opera manager in any city of the world who, single-handed and under circumstances of such difficulty, would have risked his fortune in opera. His pluck appealed to me from the first, and I leave as I came, his loyal friend and admirer.

The end of both seasons, Hammerstein's and the Met.'s, in mid April precipitated an explosion of bids and counter-bids for the stars, with clauses and sub-clauses of a complexity rivalling the (totally convincing) scene in the Marx Brothers' film *A Night at the Opera* – as an example, Bonci's contract specified payment in gold coin, to be deposited in a particular bank in Florence, but only by an 'Italian citizen'. Hammerstein got Madame Nordica by paying her at least seventeen hundred and fifty dollars a show, while the Met. bribed Bonci to desert Hammerstein for fifteen hundred.

At the same time, each house dropped their failures, and Hammerstein went so far as to take the invariably hazardous course of trying to persuade the stouter singers to adjust their shape. When he poked Signor Ancona in the belly and suggested that he should lose two stone if he wanted his contract to be renewed, the outraged tenor replied: 'That not fat, that my CHEST!'

What must have been particularly satisfying to Hammerstein's family was that the audited accounts of the Manhattan Opera's first season showed a profit of a hundred and ten thousand dollars on a turnover of seven hundred and fifty thousand, as against the Met.'s loss of nearly eighty-five thousand. So it was with justifiable confidence that Hammerstein announced he would be sailing for Europe to recruit talent for his new season. It was as well that he had made himself into such a familiar sight, for he left his ticket behind, locked in a safe. When challenged by the purser, he flourished his hat – 'No one else wears a hat like mine!' One look was enough to convince: he was allowed to sail.

The main object of this trip was Mary Garden, the thirty-year-old Aberdeen-born soprano now based in Paris whose singing of the French repertoire, particularly of Louise and Mélisande, had made her world famous. As usual, Hammerstein was only too anxious to fit in with whatever she wanted – she should sing what she liked, with whomever she liked – even to the point of granting her a veto over the props and décor of any opera she was in. His single stipulation was that this accommodation of her wishes should be subject only to maintaining Campanini's role as Musical Director.

Hammerstein even went so far as to take his first trip in a motor-car – with Mary Garden at the wheel. This, a visit to Fontainebleau, nearly ended in disaster, not because they crashed (as they did, when a wheel fell off, ending up in a poppy field), but because the incident was reported in the New York press, thus alerting the Met. to the possibility that Garden might join their rival enterprise. Conreid immediately cabled to recruit Garden himself, but it was too late: she had signed with Hammerstein. He then moved on to Berlin to negotiate with Richard Strauss over presenting *Elektra*, and his proposal to trump the Met. with a successful re-presentation of *Salome*.

Returning from Europe, Hammerstein now embarked on the dangerous course of extending his work outside New York. His first choice was Philadelphia, as being conveniently close to New York and a city of culture with an already developed taste for grand opera. His original suggestion had been that a consortium should build a suitable theatre in which his company would come and perform. When this failed to stimulate any noticeable response he decided, characteristically, that he would simply have to build the thing himself.

Back in New York, he opened the Manhattan's second season with Lillian Nordica singing the title role in *La Gioconda* on 4 November 1907, immediately followed by *La Damnation de Faust*. Much concentration had previously been devoted to taunting his rivals at the Met. with empty announcements that Melba would be coming back, or that a great Wagner season (their speciality) was on its way.

In addition to the Woolworth loan, the box office had taken a hundred and seventy-five thousand dollars in advance bookings (nearly three and half times the previous year's total), much of this the result of 'society' support of the sort Hammerstein so deeply disliked. Foremost among those encouraging their friends to subscribe was a Mrs Clarence Mackay. The *New York Times*, reporting on the *Gioconda* opening, mentions that Mary Garden was in a stage box with her father and sister, and that the Duchess of Marlborough (Consuelo Vanderbilt, daughter of the man who founded the Met. and thus a significant presence at its rival) and her diamonds were in Mrs Mackay's box.

Having signed on more stars than he needed, Hammerstein fell back on his previous practice of quarrelling with those whom he could do without, provoking them to quit so that he could avoid having to pay their agreed fees. Artists mistreated by him in this way included Madame Nordica, and even Calvé.

Nordica was now forty-eight, and perceptibly less attractive to audiences. He had signed for her to give thirty performances at two thousand dollars a show, partly as an insurance against any failure of his French plans with Garden. Now he had no need of her: knowing of her natural distaste for cigar smoke, he went out of his way to blow clouds of smoke at or near her from his usual position beside the stage. When he followed this by proposing a series of café-concerts with her as the principal *chanteuse*, she had had enough, and broke her contract, saving him approximately fifty thousand dollars. With lesser lights he was even less chivalrous. He finally agreed to hear a young soprano who had threatened suicide after being refused an audition; having heard her sing he opened a drawer and, without a word, handed her a revolver.

Friday 22 November, the day planned for Mary Garden's début, was the sort of day the public enjoy hearing about. Hammerstein, understandably excited, with all the seats sold and the critics poised, called on her, only to be told that she had lost her voice. Aghast, he argued ... she sang a note ... he realised there was nothing to be done. Hastily summoning the cast of *Les Contes d'Hoffmann*, he made an announcement from the stage to an astonished audience: the opera was to be changed, and anyone wishing to leave would have their money refunded. It was an object lesson in one of the iron rules of the business: no star, no show.

Garden sang the second performance – to mixed reviews, since the French 'sound' took some by surprise – and immediately succumbed again. But Clarence Mackay, accompanying his wife as she pursued her new interest, sent a message by way of Arthur Hammerstein that if Hammerstein senior ever found himself in financial difficulties, he (Mackay) would be happy to underwrite the company. Hammerstein's curmudgeonly answer to this munificent offer was to send back a message telling him 'to go to hell!' It was prudently suppressed by Arthur, and a more courteous refusal substituted. The skills and the attitude of mind needed to cow and control the rampant egos of an opera cast were not necessarily those best suited to the flattering of ambitious sponsors.

These two factors by themselves – his obsessive distaste for 'society' support, and his continuing aggressive attitude to the big names whom he had come to resent – might have been enough to undermine the Manhattan seriously even without Hammerstein's third and easily predictable 'own goal': his decision to build an opera house in Philadelphia.

The orchestra meanwhile, rehearsed to the point of exhaustion by the increasingly perfectionist Campanini, went on strike, and Campanini himself announced that he was returning to Italy. Scarcely had Hammerstein calmed down both parties before he was in the middle of another of his wild successes, the début of Campanini's sister-in-law, the Florentine coloratura soprano Luisa Tetrazzini, as Violetta. Tetrazzini had originally been under contract to sing for Conreid at the Met. after a modest success in San Francisco, but he had allowed her contract to lapse. The hysteria in London following her Lucia had turned her into a hot property, but by that time it was too late. This disappointment was the final straw for the embattled Conreid: on 12 February the Met. announced that he would leave in six weeks, at the end of the season.

Much admired by her fellow prima donnas Patti and Garden (perhaps because she hardly challenged them in looks), Tetrazzini's voice was acidly described by one critic as sounding like 'some incredibly perfected mechanical toy'. Whatever the truth of the matter, she had a history of driving audiences to frenzy, an ability which is in no way indicated by her surviving photographs but which was no doubt much assisted by her ringing top E flats, which she sprinkled like stardust among her arias.

The New York audiences were still recovering from this popular triumph when Hammerstein presented them with Mary Garden in *Pelléas et Mélisande*, an opera as far from *Traviata* as it was then possible to find, in its ruthless rejection of both charm and melody. But Hammerstein was on a roll, and despite some misgivings about the music, the audience responded with acclaim. When Garden dragged the familiar figure out into the spotlight, he spoke from the heart:

If a work of such sublime poetry and musical grandeur meets with your approbation and receives your support, it places New York at the head of cities of musical culture throughout the world. As for myself, I have had but one object in presenting the opera – to endear myself to you and to perpetuate myself in your memory.

At the end of the Manhattan's second season, Arthur Hammerstein calculated his father's profit at two hundred and fifty thousand dollars. The Met. had lost nearly a hundred thousand, and Otto Kahn was in the process of secret negotiations to replace Conreid with Giulio Gatti-Casazza (for ten years previously the vigorous new-broom *intendant* at La Scala, Milan), on condition that he bring his colleague Toscanini with him as Musical Director. The battle in New York was about to enter a new phase, but Hammerstein was mentally involved elsewhere.

Philadelphia, just a couple of hours south of New York by train, had a tradition of receiving visits by the Met. on Tuesdays. Vincent Sheean speculates that Hammerstein's motivation in expanding to Philadelphia, an apparently pointless move given that the city already had an adequate provision of first-class opera, many have been a desire to achieve nothing short of a total domination of opera presentation in North America by smashing the Met. This would certainly introduce an agreeably business-like element into the explanation for his ruin, but unfortunately the theory leaves out of account Hammerstein's actions before, in Harlem, and afterwards, in London – for which there can be no explanation but that he had a mania for presenting opera, regardless of the consequences.

That March, giving a visiting performance of *Louise* at Philadelphia's Academy of Music, Hammerstein came out on the stage after the curtain calls and announced that he was about to build and open a new opera house on Broad Street.

What was more, it would open later that year, on 15 November.

Arthur, peacefully unaware of his father's plans until that announcement, had to cancel a planned trip to Europe with his family. Instead, with his usual attitude of resigned but faithful co-operation in his incorrigible father's plans, he hired the necessary labourers, and by 1 April had begun the job of dismantling the old Harrah mansion which stood on the site his father had secretly bought.

Wonderfully phlegmatic in contrast to his mercurial parent, Arthur calmly settled down to his terrific task. He ordered seven million hard-pressed bricks in addition to the two million salvaged from the mansion, plus twenty thousand tons of structural steel. While he waited for the materials to be delivered he had a hole dug, eighteen feet deep and the size of a city block. The first concrete for the foundations was poured on 1 June, the first steel column was raised on 24 June, and the following day Hammerstein laid the corner-stone and deposited in the foundations a box which contained photographs and recordings of many of his principals, including Garden, Melba, Tetrazzini ... and Oscar Hammerstein. By 17 August the roof was on. To pay for all this, Hammerstein sold his Lew M. Fields theatre on 42nd Street in New York, for two hundred and twenty-five thousand dollars.

Yet the first crack in the Hammerstein façade had already appeared. On the eve of the corner-stone ceremony, an uncharacteristically shrill message from him published in the *Philadelphia Public Ledger* threatened to cancel the opera season and present vaudeville instead if he did not receive more support, by way of advance sales and box subscriptions, from Philadelphia society. Perhaps the day would have been saved nevertheless if it had been ignored; instead, there was a concerted effort to support him, led by a form of voting lottery, with tickets in the stalls as prizes, published and organised by the *North American*. Advance sales soared; Philadelphia was to get its Hammerstein grand opera after all.

Meanwhile he was again in London, in Paris, in Berlin, negotiating for his third season, which was again to include Melba, Garden and Tetrazzini. When the *Lorraine* docked at New York on 31 October 1908, Hammerstein was there to greet his new artistes – and there too was Gatti-Casazza, the new manager of the Met., to meet a second contingent. It all made splendid copy for the press, and was excellent news for New York's opera audience, and for their fellow-fans in Philadelphia.

The Manhattan opened first, on 9 November, with *Tosca*, and with Mrs Clarence Mackay entertaining Lord and Lady Northcliffe in her box. This was followed by Garden in *Thaïs*, then by Tetrazzini as Rosina in *Il Barbiere di Siviglia* on the Saturday. What a week for the archivists!

And then, the following Tuesday, the Philadelphia Opera House opened, as promised, with Maria Labia, Charles Dalmorès and Maurice Renaud in *Carmen*. Not only were all the seats sold, but an extra two thousand people were crammed into the aisles and at the back, producing an audience of more than six thousand – and this on a night when the Met. were presenting *La Bohème* with Caruso on the other side of town. At the end of the show, the audience stood and cheered while the chorus lifted Hammerstein onto their shoulders and paraded him up and down the stage.

After such a start there was no holding him, and he hired three special trains to shuttle his productions back and forth. With the Met. using the same line, life at the recently opened Penn Station must have been more than usually colourful.

Melba 'came out of retirement' for *La Bohème*. Garden, one of her greatest fans, gave an intense *Salome*. She studied for and performed the dance herself, following a lunch with Strauss during which he pointed out that he had given the soprano a ten-minute rest before the climax specifically to enable her to perform the role in full. Judged against the Met.'s half-hearted effort the year before, this was another triumph. Hammerstein had made a point of inviting numerous clergymen to the show, and their indignant refusals were grist to the already inflamed publicity mill, ensuring that all his ten performances were sold out.

But Nemesis was now standing in the wings. At the Manhattan alone, Arthur reckoned his father's expenses as follows:

Tetrazzini	40 shows @ $1,500	$60,000
Renaud	40 shows @ $1,200	$48,000
Sammarco	40 shows @ $1,200	$48,000
Garden	20 shows @ $1,400	$28,000
Melba	20 shows @ $3,000	$60,000
Other principals:		$245,000
Orchestra (85)	25 wks @ $6,000	$150,000
Conductors:		
Campanini	" $1,000	$25,000
De La Fuente	" $500	$12,500
Anselmi	" $300	$7,500
Chorus	" $2,000	$50,000
Ballet	" $700	$17,500
Stagehands	" $3,000	$75,000
Scenery storage	" $700	$17,500
Scenery movement	" $1,000	$25,000
Front of house	21 wks @ $2,500	$52,500
		$921,500

Add a rough figure of $65,000 to cover travel from Europe, buildings insurance and mortgage repayments, and it can be seen that the addition of Philadelphia (resulting in Hammerstein having to present four shows on a Saturday – two there and two at the Manhattan) must have pushed his expenditure well over one and a quarter million dollars in 1908, or more than sixty thousand a week for the twenty weeks of actual performances, as against a maximum take (a hundred per cent ticket sales) at the Manhattan of eighty thousand a week plus the catering profits he had learned to maximise from his days with Koster and Bial. The real tragedy is that the Manhattan on its own was a viable business venture, given continued support from the Mackay circle and no deterioration from the previously high standards of performance.

But Philadelphia, which had before been getting opera on a Tuesday night, was now getting it on two nights a week from the Met. and on five nights a week from Hammerstein. His money was pouring out there, and it was not pouring in. The *Philadelphia Public Ledger* for 7 January 1909 gives his weekly income as varying between thirty-two thousand in the first week and something short of twenty-five thousand in the week of 22 December. Sheean believes Hammerstein to have been in deficit in Philadelphia from the second night onwards.

It became imperative for him to raise capital, but his claims that the Philadelphia building was worth one and a quarter million dollars were met with some scepticism – well justified, as it had cost him only six hundred thousand – and the various bankers approached for a mortgage (he was looking for four hundred thousand dollars on top of the existing two hundred thousand borrowed against the site) all required the Manhattan Opera house to be added in as additional collateral. This infuriated the increasingly mercurial Hammerstein, who suddenly announced that he would cease to present opera in Philadelphia on 23 January 1909, devoting the house thereafter to what the *Philadelphia Public Ledger* described as 'negro minstrels and performing dogs, clog dancing and comedy-sketches'. Naturally this provoked uproar, and even Melba weighed in, haranguing her audience at the curtain call and demanding that they support Hammerstein. The result of all this was that he got his four hundred thousand dollar mortgage, but from a dangerous source: E. T. Stotesbury, *éminence grise* of the New York Met. and a man whose money-pots needed to be dipped into with a very long spoon indeed.

Meanwhile, back at the Met. the directors, humiliated by the successes of Hammerstein and especially by the unflattering comparisons of their conductors with Campanini, were expending both money and effort on a musical rebirth. Indeed they overdid it, and had both Mahler and Toscanini competing angrily to conduct works which each considered his own especial domain. This of course stimulated Campanini to demand longer and longer rehearsal time to compete with such distinguished rivals.

At this point, on 10 January 1909, the Clarence Mackays gave a grand party. As we saw, Arthur had not delivered his father's ludicrously insulting reply to their previous offer of financial backing, and they had continued to drum up trade among their friends, accounting in all for perhaps a quarter of the regular subscribers. This being the case, when they asked whether Campanini and the Manhattan Opera orchestra would 'drop in' after the evening's performance to play Debussy's 'La Mer', Arthur managed to persuade his father to agree. Hammerstein even sent a note to say that they would play 'with his compliments' – that is, without charge – although nothing would have persuaded him to attend.

The party was a great success without him, and the Mackays distributed generous presents to everyone who had played, including a five thousand dollar ring to Campanini. There was nothing for Hammerstein: not only was he 'the boss', but he had not even replied to their invitation. When Hammerstein heard of this, he completely lost control. Was it from jealousy of Campanini? Increasing anger at his costly demands for more rehearsal time? Simple pique at feeling excluded? More irrational distaste for 'society'? Most likely it was the result of a curdled accumulation of all four.

Hammerstein wrote a letter to Mrs Mackay, telling her never to enter his opera house again. Arthur, compounding his previous deception, destroyed it. Confronted by his parent, Arthur said that he could not and would not deliver such a disastrous letter to someone who had worked so hard to help his father in his endeavours. So Hammerstein wrote a second letter, and delivered it himself.

Those whom the Gods wish to destroy, they first make mad. Campanini resigned. The Mackays and their friends shunned the Manhattan. Where previously the rows of seats were full of enthusiastic patrons, now there were awkward gaps, and nothing accelerates faster than failure. Yet Hammerstein was off buying up new sites, paying a hundred and sixty thousand dollars for one in Brooklyn and acquiring others in Cleveland and Boston. He also took his company on tour, to Boston, Pittsburgh and Chicago. It is clear now, with hindsight, and must have been clear then to Arthur at least, that Hammerstein had finally lost all touch with reality. He had achieved so much, then had proceeded to throw it away unnecessarily, perhaps out of arrogance, more probably in his habitual disregard for conventional caution. From now on he was operating in a vacuum as far as any capacity for rational decision-making was concerned, though outwardly no doubt he still seemed the same old Hammerstein, if not more so – the Comic of Times Square, the Wizard of Opera.

Disaster was in the air, but Hammerstein was sniffing the pure oxygen of fantasy. Sadly, this also extended to his personal life, where his open pursuit of small but pneumatic contraltos was becoming increasingly unseemly, if only because of his marked lack of success. One, a Mrs Salter from Denver, made public some of his five hundred love letters to her (all beginning 'My dearest darling Boozie') in an attempt to winkle damages out of him for allegedly going back on a promise to promote her singing career. They make sad reading, but Hammerstein was splendidly robust in out-facing their widespread publication:

Yes, I wrote them. I don't try to squirm out of anything. What's more I meant every word I wrote. Can't a man write love letters? I wanted to and I did.

And so on. She sued him for a hundred thousand dollars, but the case was settled out of court.

Despite all the distractions, the Manhattan finished its third (1908) season with a profit of nearly two hundred and thirty thousand dollars, though this has to be set against the very large but unquantified losses made in Philadelphia. The shadowy E. T. Stotesbury is recorded as having lent Hammerstein sixty-seven thousand, ostensibly to help cover the season's deficit, on top of the mortgage.

The Met., by contrast, had lost more than two hundred thousand dollars, or a total of more than four hundred thousand (thirty-two million dollars in today's terms) in the three years of the rivalry, and no one – not even the Vanderbilts, let alone the astute and business-like Otto Kahn – could accept that with equanimity, especially on a continuing basis.

The banker Otto Kahn was a new figure in the Met. establishment. After years of exclusion – as a Jew he was originally debarred from taking a box there – he had bought some of the stock and joined the Board in 1907. As early as December 1908 he had approached Arthur to discuss the relations between the two rival houses. As an enthusiastic attender of Hammerstein's performances he was, perhaps, in a stronger position to make such an approach than, say, Vanderbilt himself. What may have been more to the point, Kahn's close associate, the aptly named Stotesbury, held Hammerstein's mortgage on the new Philadelphia Opera House, and other debts.

Hammerstein's fourth season at the Manhattan and his second in Philadelphia opened on 8 November 1909 with the barefoot-orange-seller-turned-international-starlet Lina Cavalieri as Massenet's Hérodiade. His engagement of Cavalieri, famed for her great beauty and her compliant if expensive nature as much as for the smallness of her voice, gave an additional cause for ill-feeling on the part of the Met. Veteran of an affair with the Russian Prince Alexander Bariatinsky and, she claimed, eight hundred and forty proposals, Cavalieri had married an Astor fledgling and subsequently been paid off by his outraged parents at huge expense. Now, with money to burn, she was being hotly pursued by one of the Vanderbilt boys, thus making her 'Least-Favoured Soprano' as far as the anxious parents of susceptible offspring among the Met. establishment were concerned. Casting her did not help Hammerstein much with Mary Garden, either. Hérodiade was followed the next night by Tetrazzini and the twenty-five year old John McCormack in *Lucia di Lammermoor*.

With Garden already preparing *Sapho* and Mazarin her astounding *Elektra* (she had actually worked in an insane asylum), it appeared to be business as usual for Hammerstein and the Manhattan: a stimulating and innovatory repertoire with some fine international stars in the casts. But behind the glossy façade, the ugly truth was that bankruptcy was weeks rather than months away. Kahn's initial discussions were based on the idea of a merger, perhaps even with Hammerstein (for whom he always professed great affection and admiration, even though the two men never met face to face) in charge. But on 9 December Kahn telephoned Arthur to tell him that the animosity felt at the Met. against his father was too great to allow for any degree of co-operation. No doubt Hammerstein's persistent gibes had hit home, not to mention his bringing the brazen if delicious Madame Cavalieri to New York.

Unbelievably, Hammerstein chose this moment to initiate a new operation in Pittsburgh, opening on 20 December with Tetrazzini and John McCormack in *Lucia*. In addition, he sent a large group under the conductor Alfred Haakman off on an eleven-week tour of Canada. They travelled in a special train with seven coaches, giving a repertoire of light French operetta together with *Mignon*, *Lucia*, *Carmen* and *Faust*. Their first night was in Montreal on 13 December. By the time they were disbanded, on 31 January 1910, the tour had lost forty thousand dollars.

Meanwhile, back in New York, an approach was made on 15

December through a mutual friend, Lee Shubert, with the suggestion that the Met. might buy Hammerstein out. This was repeated on the 18th, and indignantly rejected by Hammerstein, for whom the inescapable message of his plunging accounts was too grim to be faced. His Pittsburgh expedition had moved on to Cincinnati, where Tetrazzini, expected to sing Violetta, went down with a throat infection, causing the ticket-holders to bombard the box office, demanding refunds. The performance of *Traviata* went ahead, to an almost empty house, with McCormack as Alfredo. The *Cincinnati Enquirer* recorded on 29 December that 'a gloom as thick as the proverbial London fog settled over the hall' – matched no doubt by a similar reaction in Hammerstein's office.

Naturally there was much rumour and speculation about all this, and on 4 January the Met. issued a press statement, signed by Vanderbilt, Clarence Mackay and Otto Kahn, that 'no negotiations have been pending or are now pending between Mr Hammerstein's opera company and the Metropolitan'. No one believed this, especially after Arthur Hammerstein countered with a press statement of his own, detailing all the Met.'s recent proposals. It was, of course, the signal for the real talking to begin, not least because Hammerstein's operating deficit for the Philadelphia season proved to be just over a hundred thousand dollars. On 11 April Hammerstein was in Stotesbury's Philadelphia office, where the latter was ostensibly co-ordinating a meeting (it was ultimately unsuccessful) designed to secure full funding for Hammerstein's next season there.

As his father's factotum, Arthur Hammerstein's role in the past had been principally to carry out whatever new demand was made of him – for example, the total construction and fitting out of the four-thousand-seater Philadelphia Opera House in seven months – with the minimum fuss. Now, at the gravest crisis, he took control. His father was peremptorily ordered to go to Paris, and to wait there for further news. The surprising thing is that he obeyed. He signed a deed on 15 April giving Arthur Power of Attorney to make the best deal he could, and sailed for France the following day.

The deal which Arthur and Kahn concocted, and which was signed in Kahn's house on 26 April, was a generous one, so generous that the reason for it has never been satisfactorily explained.

Basically, the Met. took over Hammerstein's existing commitments, such as his outstanding contracts with singers, and paid him twelve hundred thousand dollars in six equal monthly instalments in return for (a) his United States opera rights, his scores and his scenery; (b) a formal contract preventing Hammerstein and his son Arthur from presenting 'grand opera' in New York, Philadelphia, Chicago and Boston for ten years; and (c) the cession of the Philadelphia Opera House to Stotesbury. In theory, therefore, Hammerstein was left with the Manhattan Theater (for vaudeville), together with eight hundred thousand dollars minus his other debts to Stotesbury, which left him with around six hundred thousand dollars, in cash, coming in steadily over the next six months.

There is no doubt that to Hammerstein's family this must have seemed like the proverbial fairy-tale ending. The alternative was immediate bankruptcy, and many people questioned Kahn's motives (since it was rightly assumed that he had put up the cash) for such personal generosity. Was it out of a disinterested admiration for Hammerstein? Was it for the good name of opera? Or was it to enhance Kahn's own reputation as a great patron of the arts? There is a fourth alternative: given that the Philadelphia theatre had itself cost six hundred thousand dollars, that Hammerstein had invested many thousands of dollars in securing US performance rights, and that the Met.'s losses were currently two hundred thousand a year, and rising, it begins to seem in retrospect, as it may have seemed to Kahn at the time, like a perfectly viable deal.

What is not entirely clear is why Kahn did not just wait for Hammerstein to go under, in the hope of getting a better deal in a 'fire-sale'. But by doing it this way, the Met. acquired the services of those artists already under contract to Hammerstein, or at any rate of those they wanted to keep: the others were left to sue for what they could get on the basis of whatever hard evidence of contractual rights they could muster. Most drifted angrily away.

A jubilant Arthur showed the first cheque for a hundred thousand dollars to his incredulous brother William; then, half-drunk with relief and champagne, they sent a cable to their father, still exiled in Paris, so full of detail that it cost seven hundred dollars. When Arthur himself followed the telegram, he reports, his father greeted him, Toad of Toad Hall-like, with the words: 'This is great! On receipt of your cablegram stating you had closed the deal, I bought a piece of property on the Kingsway in London, on which to build an opera house.'

Arthur, who had loyally and patiently supported his father's increasing megalomania to his own family's increasing detriment, and now had crossed the Atlantic to give Hammerstein details of this last-minute release from disaster, reports that his immediate shocked reply was: 'I'll never talk to you again as long as I live.' Still smarting, he returned at once to New York.

And yet, should it really have been such a surprise? It is only by logical observers, watching from un-mortgaged sidelines, that a bankrupt's position is seen as impossible. And how many great fortunes are made without taking great risks? Hammerstein had risen, by his own efforts, to a position of great public eminence and private affluence. Twice before he had seen depths of disaster turn into even more dizzying heights of success. He probably saw this payment as the entirely natural result of his labours, rather than as a rich man's generous salute to a gifted loser.

Nor is diversification (almost always a mistake in the long run) an unusual manoeuvre. Tobacco manufacturers buy insurance companies, banks buy estate agencies, all in the name of spreading the risk or cutting costs, but many find that to lose money in an alien business is easier than they had expected. Hammerstein at least stayed true to his dream; in choosing London, rather than, say, San Francisco, however, he made two strategic mistakes.

First, London was already awash with opera, thanks to the rivalry between Thomas Beecham and the usual syndicate at Covent Garden. During the (summer) Season Covent Garden employed the big stars, like Melba, Tetrazzini, Dalmorès, McCormack and Sammarco; and Thomas Beechem was also at Covent Garden, as well as at His Majesty's and Drury Lane, with a rich popular repertoire including *Carmen, Elektra, Don Giovanni, Les Contes d'Hoffmann, Pelléas, Tristan* and *Figaro*; second, given Hammerstein's contempt for 'society' and his unquenchable confidence in his own judgement, he was the very last person likely to prosper in a country unfamiliar to him and where respect for, and the active support of, the social hierarchy was essential to operatic success.

The choice of Kingsway, a slum clearance site alongside the recently completed new boulevard, was either the first of many miscalculations made by a man out of his depth, or a nostalgic touch of his hat in the direction of his original investment in Harlem. Just far enough out of the mainstream then, as it still is, to be unfashionable, but central enough to be expensive, the Kingsway project was doomed from the start. But for Hammerstein it meant business as usual, hiring builders and singers, and negotiating the necessary extra finance through Rothschilds'.

By the end of 1910, a huge hoarding had been erected in front of the Kingsway site, which was between Portugal Street and Batavia Street. Behind it, work had already started on the foundations, and stuck onto the front of it was a massive poster which read:

On this site the London Opera House
is to be erected by
Oscar Hammerstein,
Builder of Opera Houses.

This was not an approach best calculated to appeal to conservative, self-effacing London Society.

The site itself Hammerstein had acquired for a ground rent of forty-eight hundred pounds a year for ninety-nine years. That was the easy part. With his main singers, like Garden, now transferred under contract to the Met., he had to start new auditions as well as supervise the building of the theatre and the planning of the productions and scenery: in short, Hammerstein was in heaven! Interviewed by the press and asked how he found the opera business, he replied, with wry self-knowledge: 'Opera's not a business. It's a disease.'

As usual the building (subsequently renamed the Stoll Theatre, and finally demolished in 1957) was to be state-of-the-art, with its own artesian well, *two* Royal entrances – one for King George V and Queen Mary, the other for the Dowager Queen Alexandra, but with the unusual additional feature of an imposing life-sized statue of Hammerstein himself, poised above anyone using them – and its very own 'Marconi apparatus' on the roof, to take last-minute bookings from tycoons similarly equipped, 'even six hundred miles out at sea'. Also as usual, it had a spectacular staircase, and was decorated in white and gold.

The theatre opened on 11 November 1911 with Nougès' *Quo Vadis?*, with Renaud as Petronius, a great spectacle which was long on lions and short on good tunes. Unfortunately, the King and Queen had left on the 9th for India, where they were to be crowned Emperor and Empress at the Great Durbar, and Queen Alexandra was otherwise engaged. Both Royal entrances were, therefore, left unused. But Hammerstein himself was in place – the kitchen chair, the hat, the coat, even the cigar; yet somehow it seemed to matter less in London than it had in New York. In the latter, he was an institution; in the former, he was something nearer a sideshow.

In place of royalty, he had the (Vanderbilt) Duchess of Marlborough, the American Ambassador, Mrs John Jacob

Astor and Prince Nicholas of Greece, together with an encouraging wodge of London 'society'. As first nights go, it was judged a success. *The Times*'s review was very fulsome on the social front, if a little guarded as to the musical merits, adding:

> Mr Hammerstein's speech at the end of the Third Act was short and to the point. 'I thank you for this flattering reception. All I wish to deserve is your respect, your friendship and your admiration.' Everyone in the house seemed ready to assure him that he already possessed all three.

His shows continued to be run smoothly if unspectacularly until, on 25 November, he presented the unknown, petite and extremely pretty Felice Lyne as Gilda in *Rigoletto*. Hers was an overnight success based more on looks than volume, but none the less gratifying to Hammerstein, who needed to take six thousand pounds a week, every week, to cover his costs. Having taken ten thousand in the opening week, and fortified by a three hundred and fifty thousand dollar mortgage negotiated by the opera-loving Alfred de Rothschild through his family bank, Hammerstein was understandably ebullient.

His first season ran from November to March, a time when his only potential rival, Covent Garden, was in abeyance – Beecham having very sensibly decided to retire temporarily from what was bound to be a surfeited market. His repertoire consisted of *Quo Vadis?*, *William Tell*, *Norma* (using some of the same set as *Quo Vadis?*), *Rigoletto*, *Faust*, *Lucia di Lammermoor*, *Hérodiade*, *Les Contes d'Hoffmann*, *Louise*, *La Traviata*, *Il Barbiere di Siviglia* and *Le Jongleur de Notre-Dame*, a kaleidoscope of operatic hits that any modern house would be proud of. The production of *Hérodiade* caused dreadful trouble, because his current object of hopeless pursuit, Marguerite d'Alvarez, the red-hot Peruvian contralto (who as Dalilah once memorably tumbled all the way down the steps of the massive Temple of Dagon in Chicago, executed a perfect forward roll and came up still singing and still on pitch), was given exaggerated top billing over the more popular and notably touchy Madame Cavalieri. Despite such an apparently fool-proof programme, however, the box-office receipts were already showing a worrying decline, and on 5 February 1912, against all conventional experience and practice, he halved the price of a stalls seat to half a guinea. This did nothing to assist his cash-flow, but a great deal to raise questions about the viability of his venture.

Hammerstein's second season, opening on 22 April, just two days behind Covent Garden, contained some revivals, and the following new shows: *Les Cloches de Corneville*, *Don Quichotte*, *Mignon* (more popular then than now), *La Favorite*, *Il Trovatore* and, crucially, *The Children of the Don*. This egregious piece, written under a pseudonym by Lord Howard de Walden, was the price Hammerstein had to pay, reluctantly, for accepting, also reluctantly, the generous support of The Committee for the Welfare of the London Opera. This, an informal group of well-wishers put together by the Duchess of Marlborough and Lord Howard de Walden, with the titular support of the Duke of Norfolk and Duke of Argyll, was exactly the sort of social support system that could have kept Hammerstein in cigars and contraltos for several years. Unfortunately, it was also exactly the sort of thing he hated. And indeed, there was very little point in rudely rejecting the kindly proferred support of the Mackays in New York if he was then going to knuckle under to the Howard de Waldens in London.

Nor was Hammerstein much more accommodating to the monarchy. Persuaded that a Royal Visit was essential, he stood bare-headed in the foyer to meet the new Emperor and Empress, a man beside him hanging on tightly to his hat, which it had been thought he might 'forget' to remove. No such forethought had been given to the cigar, however, and it remained firmly in place during what became a famous exchange, much discussed in polite society. King George V and Queen Mary had insisted on using the public entrance (possibly on account

of the controversial statue), and found the strange figure waiting
for them, wreathed in smoke:

> *Hammerstein (abruptly, without waiting to be presented):*
> How are you, King? I'm glad to see you.

> *George V:* I'm delighted to meet you, Mister Hammerstein.
> I admire your theatre very much.

It was generally agreed that the King had the better of this
exchange, a matter of small consolation to the dismayed
members of the Welfare Committee. The Royal Visit was not
repeated.

Nor was all well on other fronts. Madame d'Alvarez had left
the country to evade Hammerstein's importunities, the
American soprano Felice Lyne had slapped his face for delay-
ing a rehearsal, and he had peremptorily ordered Lady Cunard
and her party (which included the King of Portugal) out of her
box for talking during a performance.

To add to this catalogue of personal disasters, Caruso was
singing in *Madama Butterfly* at Covent Garden to massive
popular acclaim, while Hammerstein's takings on the first night
of *Don Quichotte* were just eighty-five pounds (excluding the subscriptions), and fell to fifty-one pounds on subsequent nights.

The final straw was *The Children of the Don*. One can imagine
Hammerstein's accelerating chagrin at having to be involved in
the presentation of a long maundering verse-drama of impen-
etrable Druidic mythology with no discernible on-stage action
at all. *The Times* review described it as 'probably the most severe
blow which the cause of struggling English opera has sustained
for many years'.

When Lord Howard de Walden, who no doubt had already
paid dearly for the four contracted performances of his only
known work, asked shyly ... um ... er ... what a fifth performance might cost, Hammerstein thundered 'FOUR
THOUSAND POUNDS!' (an insultingly outrageous amount)

and stormed off, slamming his office door on both his chief benefactor and his London venture. For this was to be his final error of judgement. Abruptly deprived of Lord Howard de Walden's sponsorship, and with the Rothschilds becoming ever more restless about their mortgage, he announced from the stage on the Grand Gala Night of 15 July that he had personally lost forty-five thousand pounds on the season, but that he would re-open in November.

This was to be one date Hammerstein did not keep. Arthur was summoned from New York to sell the theatre and generally try to clear up his father's latest débâcle. At sixty-five, Hammerstein was now too old, and too stubborn, to succeed at anything. It was a sad decline from the glory days before ambition and *folie de grandeur* had wrecked his judgement and set mania in the place of energy. His total losses were said to be more than a million dollars in eighteen months, and some of it must have been put up by his sons, out of their successful vaudeville profits at the New York Victoria.

Hammerstein tried to go back to the roots of his success, by devising a new formula for cheaper cigars. Then he surfaced with an idea for an opera house in Cleveland, and another in St Louis. He was now back in New York, and living in his two rooms at the Victoria, even though its revenues were closed to him.

Unfortunately the Met.'s legal adviser, Paul Cravath, told him that opera in English was not covered by the exclusion clause (Cravath was quite wrong: it was specifically excluded). This of course sparked off a new plan: The Lexington Opera House, with three thousand seats, and financed, to his family's horror, by his sale for two hundred and fifty thousand dollars of the residual rights (never passed on to his sons) to produce vaudeville in the area of New York which included their Victoria Theater.

Hammerstein's capacity to do them damage must have seemed limitless to his sons. The Lexington, though still in course of construction, was advertised with his usual optimism to open with English opera on 10 November 1913. The Met. sought and gained an injunction, and Hammerstein appealed, but on 17 April 1914 the New York Supreme Court decided unanimously in favour of the Met., and Stotesbury was back, too, weighing in with a nasty little lawsuit claiming forty thousand dollars still unpaid from the old Philadelphia mortgage. There was to be no opera, in English or in any other language, from either Oscar or Arthur Hammerstein, for ten years.

The year had started as it was to go on. Three of Hammerstein's sons, Abe, Willie and Harry, died at this time. Although Hammerstein was never a 'family man' of any description, such a disaster was crushing. Moreover, it had been Willie (a victim of the same Bright's Disease that killed Mapleson, and father of Oscar Hammerstein II who wrote *South Pacific* and *Oklahoma!*) who, with his genius for vaudeville, more than once paid to keep his father's dreams afloat. Hammerstein showed signs of faltering, yet all this time the Lexington was steadily rising above ground. It cost nearly a million and quarter dollars to build and equip. It opened on 22 August 1914 as a cinema, with Arthur in charge, but was soon sold for about two-thirds of what it had cost, and the Victoria had to be sold the same year. When all the debts were paid, Arthur bought his father a house at Atlantic Highlands in New Jersey, and here Hammerstein spent an uneasy time, nursing a septic foot which never healed. He had an operation on it in March 1915, but remained angrily dependent on crutches.

He had also been married for a third time, in January 1914, to a beautiful woman in her early thirties named Emma Swift. It was a ship-board romance, and his almost immediate operation and subsequent decline must have been a sad blow for them both. Certainly there seems no doubt that it soured their brief marriage.

There was to be one last return to the spotlight. At the Hippodrome Theater on 26 March 1916, before a gathering of

American composers, he heard Sousa introduce him as the one 'who had done more for music than any other man in America'. Not bad for a runaway boy from Stettin, he might have reflected, as he hobbled across the stage to conduct his own composition, 'The Louise Waltz', before bowing to acknowledge his last standing ovation.

He lingered on, old before his time, through 1917 and 1918, tinkering with his cigar-making equipment and talking about the operas he would present in 1920, once the Met.'s exclusion clause had expired. When Mary Garden was asked by reporters if she had heard of his plans, she said: 'If Mr Hammerstein ever wants me to sing for him again, I will be glad to do it for nothing.'

But one day in July 1919, as he drove past the station at Atlantic Highlands, Harry Rosenberg, the brother-in-law first involved more than forty years before in the Harlem Opera House, saw a familiar top hat lying on the railway platform. He stopped his car and went over, only to find Hammerstein lying unconscious behind the bench.

They took him to hospital, where he told them he had had a row with his wife, in the course of which she had emptied a bucket of cold water over him in bed. He asked that she should not be allowed into his hospital room, but she forced her way in, and stayed beside him. After a few days he fell into a coma. Still she stayed; and she was there, with Arthur, until he died, on 1 August.

In summary, Hammerstein's great success was due to his own impressive and single-minded efforts in assembling first money, and then a coherent ensemble who could be relied upon to provide high-quality performances in a world where standards varied enormously. His final and complete failure was due to his inability either to consolidate present successes before launching into further ventures, or to suppress the internal demon that drove him to quarrel unnecessarily with those who could most assist him – his successful artistes, and the rich sponsors who, treated with courtesy, could have sustained and perpetuated his ascendancy over the Met. These two contrasting sides to his character, both rooted in his awkward childhood, determined the parabolas of Hammerstein's life.

While he was building the Philadelphia Opera House, he had given a newspaper interview in which he said:

> Grand opera is more than music. It is more than drama; it is more than spectacle; it is more than social function; it is more than a display of passion, whether subdued or fierce; it is more than a song or tale of love; it is more than a series of pictures; it is all these things and more. It is the awakening of the soul to the sublime and the divine; and this is, I believe, the true mission of grand opera.

There can be little doubt that he truly believed this.

4

John Christie
(1882–1962)

JOHN CHRISTIE WAS the opposite of Oscar Hammerstein in that he was born heir to great riches, yet his childhood, like Hammerstein's, proved exceptionally unhappy.

The Christie family, originally named Christin and Swiss in origin, had inherited the large Glyndebourne estate in Sussex with its pretty Georgian manor house in 1833, after a protracted lawsuit with other cousins, also potential heirs. Furthermore, Christie's grandfather William had married Agnes Clevland, who was the heiress to another great estate, Tapeley in Devon, following the death of her brother Archibald, who had survived the Charge of the Light Brigade only to be shot at the Battle of Inkerman at the age of twenty-one. William and Agnes's eldest son, Augustus, a large man of very uncertain temperament, was therefore a matrimonial catch, being heir, according to the then widespread system of primogeniture, to the whole of both his parents' inheritances despite being the eldest of six brothers and three sisters. In February 1882 Augustus married Lady Rosamund Wallop, a daughter of Isaac, 5th Earl of Portsmouth, and the birth of their son John on 14 December should have been a cause of widespread celebration.

It seems, however, that something untoward happened between husband and wife during October, something so unfortunate that when Augustus refused to follow subsequent medical advice or indeed even to see his own father, Lady Rosamund immediately left Tapeley and eventually gave birth to their only child at Eggesford, Lord Portsmouth's house in North Devon.

If John Christie's birth was inauspicious, what followed was worse. Augustus was persuaded to go abroad, where he spent some time in Egypt and then the Crimea, first with a Doctor Hoggan and later, when Hoggan had had enough, with a Doctor Howard. There was already a distinct strain of eccentricity in the family. Augustus's father William, speaking of his wife Agnes Clevland, had once said: '[She] is I fancy a trifle mad, but not sufficiently so for me to be able to take any *definite steps* ...' Augustus added to this the physique of a prize-fighter and an unpredictable violence of temper which must have made him a very formidable and difficult presence in the family circle. Certainly his wife's letters speak frequently of his 'cruelties' and 'loss of control'.

For four years the couple lived apart. One hundred years on, such a situation would hardly be noticed, or remarked upon if it was. But late Victorian England viewed these things differently, and the pressure to conform, at least outwardly, was very strong indeed. Lady Rosamund was persuaded by her parents (Lord Portsmouth may have been a more understanding father-in-law than most, since his own uncle, the 3rd Earl, had had, like Augustus, to be confined) to return to Tapeley with her four-year-old son, and at this point a second problem arose: Augustus Christie displayed a manic jealousy of John. He could not bear to see him, nor would he allow his wife even to bath him.

All Lady Rosamund's capacity for love, therefore, turned away from her impossible husband, and settled on her only son, with the inevitable result that he became spoilt and difficult – an understandable and relatively modest reaction, upon which the manners of the times brought down a dreadful retribution: at the age of six he was sent away to boarding school, at Fremington near Barnstable.

Although he was so young, it was at this stage that Christie began to show his mettle. 'On the first night', as his mother's personal 'Reminiscences' record,

> everyone was roused by terrified howls from the dormitory. My little boy had waited until the other children were asleep, then slipped out of bed and hurried along the dormitory stripping the bedclothes off the sleeping children. We paid a bill of nineteen shillings for broken windows after his first term.

Where the young Oscar Hammerstein had rebelled against being beaten by his father, the young John Christie had to cope with being beaten by everyone. When his mother birched his hand at home, he managed to stretch it out and ask for more. At Fremington he was beaten regularly, as well as being the object of attacks by other boys (his parents had rashly sent him to the school in a Little Lord Fauntleroy outfit). At the age of ten he was moved on to board at St David's School in Reigate, where the headmaster, a Mr Churchill, had a positive relish for the cane.

In 1896, aged thirteen, Christie passed successfully into Eton where, he recalled, he was caned or birched nearly every term. All these assaults no doubt went to breed that fatalistic disdain for physical pain and danger which became evident during his service in the trenches of the Great War.

He had already begun to spend most of his holidays with his aunt, Lady Margaret Watney. She was married to the Chairman of Watney's Brewery, who subsequently bought Cornbury Park, a large country house outside Oxford. Spending so much time in Oxfordshire rather than in Devon, Christie may have been largely unaware of the awful circumstances of his parents' marriage.

John Christie (1882–1962)

Small for his age, he found at Eton and deeply appreciated the *lebensraum* which that school alone grants to even its youngest recruits. In his case it was intensely liberating. Even better, he reached the science class of the Revd Dr T. C. Porter and became a friend of the Precentor, Dr Charles Harford Lloyd, a fine organist, both of whom were able to give him the sympathetic guidance and paternal encouragement so disastrously lacking at home, and both of whom hugely influenced the course of a life divided between science (which he taught) and music (which he promoted).

At some point around his sixteenth birthday, it became agreed that the Army would be the right place for Christie, and his work thereafter, until he left Eton in July 1900, was geared towards the Woolwich (School of Artillery) entry. That this was not his own choice is shown by a letter to his mother, in which he tries to make arrangements to sell his bicycle to his father in order to buy a 'laboratory' from Baird & Tatlock's costing twenty-three pounds. He ends: 'I want to see you about giving up the Army and doing science. It is such a waste of time going into the Army.'

Nevertheless, he entered the Royal Academy, Woolwich in October 1900. In his fourth term he fell when his horse slipped at a jump in the riding school, and his foot was severely crushed. For ten days no one paid much attention. Then his mother sent her carriage and had him taken to Queen Victoria's doctor, Sir Thomas Barlow. Barlow, with the aid of science's newest invention, the X-ray, was able to reset the bones, but not to save him from a lifelong limp.

In January 1902 he wrote to his father, asking for his support if he were to leave the Army and concentrate on science, at which he promised to work hard. This appeal was successful, and by October he was an undergraduate of Trinity College, Cambridge, studying Natural Science and writing to his mother to negotiate an allowance. He also invited her to visit him, adding, 'Mind you come well-dressed.'

A new passion had become paramount: the motor-car. Originally interested in a six-horsepower Regal, he eventually bought, with much help from his mother and the Watneys, a Georges-Richard, of aluminium construction, which was delivered to Cornbury where he was staying with his aunt. From the start his driving seems to have been exceptionally erratic, and it was to remain the source of great angst to his passengers all his life. Was there just a touch of Mr Toad about John Christie? Certainly their driving techniques were strikingly similar. Childs, his long-serving butler and friend, related one occasion when the car, with Christie at the wheel, suddenly bucketed through a hedge and into a field:

'Sir, sir – you're off the road. *You're off the road*!'

'Yes, Childs, I *know*. I've seen another gap further on and I'm going back through that.'

However, this interest opened the horizons on another – opera; or, more precisely, Wagnerian opera. In the summer of 1904, with the Eton Precentor Dr Lloyd on the seat beside him and his friends George Lyttelton and R. H. Longman perched in a specially adapted cheese-crate nailed to the back of the car, he set off for Bayreuth. The car was put on a hired barge which was towed across the Channel to Calais, wallowing behind the regular steamer. It is a very great pity that an age already well-accustomed to the camera should have left no (surviving) pictorial record of this singular voyage.

Safely disembarked, the four motored across France and into Germany, along cart-tracks, through fords and forests, stopping frequently when the engine overheated and even, once, getting down and pushing their strange contraption up a steep hill. On and on they rattled, through dust so thick that it often turned the Precentor's beard white. It must have been with about equal parts of gratitude and disbelief that they finally reached Bayreuth, just in time to see the last two acts of *Parsifal*, as well as *Tristan, Tannhäuser* and all four parts of *Der Ring des Nibelungen*. At the age of only twenty-one, the essential John Christie was already formed and in clear view: mildly eccentric, musically absorbed, mechanically literate, above all a dogmatic and humorous man of strong enthusiasms who, having set himself an unlikely, even impossible, task could, by sheer grit and unswerving tunnel-vision, finish what others would never even have dreamt of starting.

While he was working hard at Cambridge he was offered a railway engineering job, but he turned it down, applying instead to return to Eton to teach science. He got the job (despite his poor record as a pupil there) and the school gave him fifty pounds to equip their new laboratory, which he was to supervise. Knowing this to be a hopelessly inadequate sum, he used an aunt's legacy (his Aunt Lizzie had died unmarried at the age of thirty-two; of his father's eight siblings, four had died in their twenties or early thirties) to add a hundred and fifty pounds of his own, while at the same time selling his car for a hundred and forty pounds and buying a replacement for three hundred. His salary at Eton was to be four hundred and fifty pounds a year, plus ten pounds from each pupil in his class. By October 1906 he had started in his first job, and he kept it, the war years apart, for the next sixteen years.

Life as an Eton master in 1906 was an agreeable one, especially with Christie's own private income to add to the already generous salary. Within two years he was sharing a 'colony' at Number 2 Common Lane with two other masters, a housekeeper, a parlourmaid and a 'boy'. He also had his own manservant, a groom (for his horses) and a chauffeur.

The best description of his teaching is to be found in a memoir provided by a colleague, the venerable Classicist A. S. F. Gow, to the Eton Drawing Master Wilfrid Blunt, and taken from the latter's excellent biography of Christie. Gow seems to be referring particularly to the years at Eton after the First World War.

John was seriously interested in the Physics that he taught at Eton, contemplated and even started a text book on the subject, and bought a lot of expensive apparatus which he subsequently presented to the school. I remember a vast rheostat and a liquid-air pump which never, I think, manufactured liquid air but was useful for inflating the tyres of John's car. I should doubt if he was a very good teacher for his expositions whether of relativity or, in later days, of the organization of Glyndebourne, were noticeably lacking in lucidity; but his pupils, like his colleagues, were fond of him and enjoyed such incidents as the arrival in Early School of John's Jeeves-like butler, Childs, to announce that Captain Christie had overslept but might be expected shortly.

(If a master was more than fifteen minutes late, the boys could have a 'run' and the master was fined.)

When he was not teaching, he was kept busy with the other sides to school life to which Assistant Masters were expected to contribute, for example cricket:

[John] had a theory [recalled another colleague, Cyril Butterwick] that if a batsman called 'No!' and then ran, he would catch the fieldsman napping. That it certainly did; but it caught his partner napping too, however carefully he explained that 'Yes!' meant 'No!' and 'No!' meant 'Yes!' The second and more complicated theory was that in running between the wickets much time was lost by turning. So his plan was to spin round three yards before reaching the crease and complete the run backwards so that the next run could be started without delay. This plan was for a time quite successful because the fieldsmen were so helpless with laughter at the sight of a massive baldish man spinning round like a teetotum that they failed to take advantage of the fact that each run took several seconds longer ...

Hearing of such an idyll from those who shared it with him makes it less surprising to learn that even after years of happy family life, and the great success of his opera house, Christie still looked back on his time at Eton as his happiest.

But two shadows intervened: the Kaiser's War, and events at home.

His grandfather had lived on at Glyndebourne while his parents lived at Tapeley, and he wrote to Christie in November 1911, proposing to give him the Saunton part of his Devon estate direct. Christie wrote to his father, politely asking his advice, and must have been surprised by the furious reaction of a man who already occupied the (larger) Tapeley portion, had recently bought Lundy Island (because he could see it from his windows), and was due to inherit Glyndebourne and another ten thousand acres as well as land in Northamptonshire and Lincolnshire:

> It is unfortunate that my father's vitality has long outlived his brain ... he has no right to ignore me ... in the meantime I will tell you in private that in my opinion my father and the ex-governess are married ...

And so on. Augustus even cast aspersions on his father's mental condition, blithely unaware of the irony.

John Christie, with extraordinary generosity, told his father that he would accept his grandfather's gift of the Saunton estate, but would hand it back to him on his grandfather's death. The only response to this was a sorrowful letter from Augustus expressing the view that he had done his best to stop John making a fool of himself.

His mother had also written to him, in December 1912, apparently intending to prepare him for his great inheritances. If so, the plan misfired, for he wrote back:

> I don't really want to become a 'country gentleman'. I have sufficient to do already. Such a mode of living, though no

doubt coveted by many people, does not appear to me to be any more attractive than my present one.

And again, in May 1914, after old William Christie had finally died, leaving Saunton to John, he wrote to her from Eton:

> This talk of riches leaves me cold. I don't really take much interest in them. They do not seem to affect the near future. Anyhow I do not wish to make myself a slave to them. I want to make use of them, rather than they of me. At present I cannot entertain the idea of giving up my work here ...

In a pleasantly amicable arrangement, Christie sold Saunton back to his father for thirty-two thousand pounds while the latter allowed his only son to occupy Glyndebourne and its estate as a weekend and holiday home. Christie immediately began to plan some major alterations at Glyndebourne, basically a simplification of the house, to which his grandfather had added some charming but characteristically bombastic Victorian additions.

But elsewhere in Europe larger maps than those of Glyndebourne and Saunton were being studied; and on Saturday 11 August 1914 the Kaiser's troop trains steamed out of Berlin, never to return. Christie, concealing his limp and an eye severely damaged playing rackets at Eton, managed to enlist as a subaltern with the 60th Rifles, the King's Royal Rifle Corps.

His army life at first seemed almost as agreeable as that at Eton:

> We are most comfortable here [he wrote from Petworth House, where the Battalion officers were billeted with Lord Leconfield], 500 men in the house and stables and twenty officers and their servants ... we dine off silver plate and all the waiters have white gloves ...

adding, with his habitual tone of disparagement of his mother's
sad gushing of love over her only child, 'I think it would be well
if you were to eliminate the sentimental strain from your letters.'

It is one of the oddities of this period of Christie's life – his
thirties – that he seems to have gone out of his way to try to be
understanding to his impossible, not to say insane, father while
constantly criticising his muddle-headed but none the less
staunch and loving mother, who was always his best (and sometimes his only) ally against his father's constant if confused sense
of hostility. (For example, Augustus Christie, convinced that his
son would be killed in the trenches, began to groom a young
nephew, Edward Le Marchant, as his heir. But of the two men
who went to fight, it was Le Marchant who was killed.)

Yet John Christie's severe abhorrence of sentimentality was
to give him unexpected strength once the regiment embarked
for France. No one, not the richest of the *jeunesse dorée* nor the
poorest recruit from Glasgow's stinking tenements, could ever
have imagined what awaited them in those sodden ditches dug,
flooded and then re-excavated, all by hand, across the plains of
Flanders.

> We don't want to lose you,
> But we think you ought to go!

What a shame those enthusiastic women could not have seen
the conditions in which the victims of their encouragement
were to die. Christie's letters to his mother present a now familiar kaleidoscope of suffering:

> Every trench I have been in has necessitated wading in places
> up to the knees in dry weather. .... Most of my men were out
> last night with other companies digging within a hundred
> yards of the firing line. Very bad place. Many bodies ten days
> old. Impossible to bury them ... Shell burst quite close, got
> me right behind the ear and in front of the right shoulder. ....

It was light before I could get my last wounded away . . . I had promised them that I would not leave before they did. This much the most horrible part. Just think of those wretched fellows, badly wounded, lying in the bottom of the trench, one of them hit twice again, for three days and nights, officers and men continually climbing over them. I did not know what to do . . . the stretcher bearers did not come . . .

One thing is quite certain: this was proper war work, and in marked contrast to the comic peace-time posturing of 'Colonel' Mapleson, or Sir Thomas Beecham's undignified indifference. But Lieutenant Christie brought a surreal touch even to his soldiering, reading Spenser aloud to his wondering troops. (He also read them Plato's *Dialogues*, and *Alice Through The Looking Glass*, but it was the Spenser they really enjoyed.) Nor was he unconcerned about arrangements at home, adding to one letter to his mother:

Your letter makes me nervous lest I may find the cooking and general household management as beastly as usual. You speak of more economy. There must be no sign of it when I come home. . . . I think you had better engage a good chef from the Café Royal for a few days.

Then came the Battle of Loos. Christie, already promoted to Captain, was now made Second-in-Command of his Battalion, which was inspected by Field-Marshal Lord Kitchener on 21 September, just before the battle started. Christie's detachment was under shell-fire from 3.50 in the morning until 6 in the evening, and he reports that he lost as many as sixty-five men.

Lieutenant Holloway, also writing home, described one part of a hectic day:

Shelling was thick and continuous . . . Christie was absolutely calm, leading out a reconnaissance in one direction and ordering entrenching in another and sitting down to write reports. At one time he stood on the edge of the crater to see what calibre the shells were ... In the afternoon, when we were sitting in the battered trenches under the same relentless shell fire [unfortunately, it was from British guns] – one man was blown to bits five yards from us – he produced from his pocket the *Faerie Queen* and read it aloud to cheer us up.

After the battle Christie was recommended for the Distinguished Service Order but, seeing his name on the list, he crossed it out himself. Nevertheless, he was awarded the Military Cross.

Meanwhile, at home, his mother had been busy writing letters, and once the facts of his physical condition – the lame leg, the all-but-blinded eye – reached the Board of Interventions, he was invalided out immediately. After six months' convalescence, he was again dividing his time between supply teaching at Eton and supervising the estate at Glyndebourne. A poignant connection between past and present is supplied by his Eton colleague A. S. F. Gow, who recalls that while they were sitting on the terrace at Glyndebourne discussing plans for the house, they could listen, 'when the wind was in the right direction, to the guns firing in Flanders'.

Nor did Christie's car sit idle: Gow accompanied him on two major expeditions. The first was to Glasgow to enquire into a strike – to them incomprehensible – on the Clyde. The party took the form of Christie driving, Gow by his side, and Childs, the butler, perched in the dickey with a barrel of oysters and a large pot of caviare. Having talked to the strike leaders and encouraged them to get back to work, they drove south again, to stay with Christie's aunt Lady Margaret Watney at Cornbury Manor for the weekend. The second expedition was made in 1919, to view the empty battlefields in France. This time Childs's major responsibility was a box of Charbonnel chocolates.

If all this seems to carry with it a strong whiff of Jeeves and

Bertie Wooster, it is important to remember that P. G. Wodehouse – like Gogol, Trollope and Anthony Powell – belongs to the 'Pre-Raphaelite' school of comedy, whose practitioners' background settings are rendered with meticulous accuracy.

Childs, devoted and Olympian butler to John Christie, best man at his wedding and godfather to his son George, was a perfect exemplar of a fine tradition that continued well into the sixties but has vanished now, along with most of the duties that made it what it was. Butlers, as a distinctive, self-perpetuating and widely-propagated breed, have, like town criers and ostlers, suddenly become creatures of a superannuated past. It is not that there is suddenly a shortage of dignified, well-educated, dedicated men like Childs; it is just that nowadays they find employment in the security industry, in fine arts, or the education service.

The post-war period, between 1918 and 1939, was the Indian summer of the country house. Gone were the politicking power-house years of the eighteenth century, gone also the elaborate social and administrative rituals of the nineteenth. What was left was a gently nostalgic world of autumnal houses still tended carefully by their inhabitants, both owners and servants, survivors trained in the more spacious Edwardian years and perfectly drawn by Wodehouse, their chief fictional historian. If John Christie's life at this period sounds like something out of Wodehouse, it is because Wodehouse was depicting the truth.

In the five years following the end of the First World War more than a third of England changed hands. Agriculture, the basic underpinning of the country house, had been in decline since the late 1880s. Cheap corn from North America had undermined first farming profits, then farm rents, and finally the base value of the land itself. Those who had continued to support their personal Blandings out of capital – or, worse, by borrowing – found themselves bailing out of an asset-turned-liability at prices lower than they had been in the reign of James I.

But three generations in which heirs had married heiresses had left the Christies in an altogether happier position, and John Christie was able to indulge that pet hobby of all rich proprietors: tinkering with the plans.

As part of a general reorganisation and rationalisation, almost a quarter of a million pounds' worth of land had been sold by the family, mainly in south Lincolnshire and east Sussex; and as there were no debts to pay off, this colossal sum gave John Christie almost unlimited scope for architectural improvements.

He began by demolishing most of the Victorian additions made at Glyndebourne, including a picturesque tower on the right of the road-side façade; he installed electricity, rebuilt the kitchen; and, crucially, he added an Organ Room, designed by Edmond Warre (son of his old Eton headmaster) and with a fine organ built by Hill, Norman & Beard to the design of Dr Lloyd, Precentor of Eton and veteran of that epic journey to Bayreuth.

The idea was that Dr Lloyd would move to Glyndebourne on his retirement, and preside over a continuous *organfest* thereafter. Dr Lloyd died, however, before the organ was finished – work which had been prolonged over several years by the problems encountered in trying to make a cathedral-sized organ work in the (comparatively) restricted space available. By 1920 Christie, now the outright owner of Glyndebourne as a result of fears for his father's health following two minor strokes, had spent thirty-eight thousand pounds on renovations, which included eight thousand on the organ.

His time at Eton was nearing its end. After sixteen years as an usher (assistant master), he was approaching the seniority of being entrusted with a 'house', one of the twenty or so establishments, each accommodating around fifty boys, which form the basis of the administration of the school. At that time, as now, junior masters began to accumulate names of prospective pupils up to twelve years before the boys actually joined the school; where it was not deemed appropriate for an assistant master to be given a house, this decision was passed on to him as soon as possible, to avoid disappointing parents.

Wilfrid Blunt, Christie's first biographer and himself an Eton master, surmised that Christie's sudden departure in 1922 was the result of the Headmaster, Dr Alington, belatedly refusing to grant him a 'house'. But it is also possible that Christie meant what he said when he wrote to his mother on 5 June 1922 to announce that 'I have more or less decided not to take a house here and to retire at the end of this Half.' If so, it would not be the only decision of his life to have been taken suddenly, and irrevocably.

At the age of forty, a former professional schoolmaster with an inherited fortune and no wife, John Christie concentrated his formidable energy on providing employment in and around Glyndebourne, this having been always his stated perception of the duty that went hand in hand with enjoyment of the pleasures of a large estate. The Glyndebourne Motor Works and the Ringmer Building Works (both companies he had started himself), three thousand acres of land taken in hand and to be farmed directly under his own control, a market garden, and a timber business based on his own Plashett Woods – all these made up a massive (and fascinating) undertaking. On top of this, he bought up the whole of the Hill, Norman & Beard organ business. As Chairman he proceeded to revolutionise its methods – which he began by engaging his own business, the Ringmer Building Works, to construct a new restaurant-cum-office space.

If one key to Christie's ultimate success as a crusading impresario was his formidable indifference to any accepted norm or barrier, another was his great success in choosing, and then in keeping on board, a wide range of talented and loyal lieutenants. Childs (butler) in charge of the pantry, Harvey (head gardener) of the grounds, Sharp and Jenkins of the Building Works, Edwards of the accounts office, Veness (head keeper) of Plashett Woods, Beard of the organ works – these men were to be joined in due course by Strasser at the piano as Chief Coach, Bing as General Manager, Busch on the podium, Ebert as director, Wilson as stage manager, and Gough as the genie of the back-stage black arts. It was Christie's genius that he was able to recruit, enable, drive on but also support, and, when it was necessary to do so, defer to, this astonishing assortment of individually strong characters, none of whom would willingly have yielded precedence to any of the others, but all of whom were employed by and owed their jobs and their chance to excel to Christie.

Nor did he apparently see them as being differentiated one from the other in any degree. Childs and Busch, Gough and Ebert – these were excellent men, all professionals in one widely-educated team. That a man like Fritz Busch, veteran Musical Director at Dresden, was regarded by Christie as the equal of the head game-keeper would have seemed to Busch an outrage; to Christie, it was the highest compliment he could have paid him.

Shrewd, bombastic, simultaneously generous and mean, genial, argumentative, kindly, occasionally infuriating, subject to capricious likes and dislikes, John Christie did not just hold views on every subject, he held *absolute certainties*, from which he could only be dislodged by the most tenacious resistance.

Isaiah Berlin, writing after Christie's death, said:

He had the single-mindedness of a secular visionary ... like every great *Intendant* in the history of opera, he displayed a degree of personal authority, indeed, of the indispensable element of *terribilità* which rivalled that of Diaghilev and Toscanini.

In 1922, however, Christie's horizons were strictly rural, and opera was something he probably thought of as being connected with 'abroad', not least because in England, now that Beecham's company was severely in decline and the Covent

Garden syndicate had disbanded, there was very little opera to be heard at all. The British National Opera Company (Beecham, still struggling to clear his debts) worked hard to give fifty-eight performances in May and June. Covent Garden then went dark again until 9 October, when the Carl Rosa troupe gave thirty-one performances in twenty-six days. And that was it. London had three months of opera, and nine months with none at all.

Two new names now to be found in the Glyndebourne visitors' book were those of Fanny Mounsey and her banker husband Johnnie, with whom she had four young children. During 1923 a close friendship flourished between Christie and the Mounseys, with the result that Glyndebourne became the joint country base and the Mounseys' town house the equivalent London base for all three.

Music formed part of the ground-work of this alliance, since both Mounseys were good pianists. Additionally, Fanny in particular was a passionate organiser, with the result that the newly-started annual Festival at Lewes (Christie's nearest shopping town) soon began to expand, thanks to support from and the use of the facilities at Glyndebourne, not least of the great organ – despite the fact that the vibration of its deepest pipes dislodged great lumps of plaster from the new Jacobethan ceiling.

With the Mounseys Christie travelled to Egypt, and to Germany, specifically to Bayreuth for Wagner, and to Munich to hear Mozart (this was Fanny's influence) in the tiny rococo gem of a theatre in the Residenz. The Mounseys had often had a professional couple, the Thornely Gibsons, come in to sing extracts from *Fidelio* in their London drawing room. Now they had travelled around Germany and had seen how opera could work well in small theatres: suddenly, opera was on Christie's agenda in a big way, and organs (and especially organists) were beginning to take a back seat. In October 1924 he began to show some interest in the Tunbridge Wells Theatre, and by early 1925 he had taken over the lease.

From Munich he was writing to his mother about new plans to present *Parsifal* and *Die Entführung aus dem Serail* in the Tunbridge Wells 'Opera House' (*sic*) in 1927. Meanwhile, he opened there in July 1925 with Shaw's play *Saint Joan* in place of the announced Gilbert & Sullivan season, which must have hit some unexpected snag. Indeed, the whole Tunbridge Wells enterprise was one on which he never welcomed discussion, and he quickly lost interest in it. Yet even in this is matter for some congratulation: Christie was not one to waste excessive time on those of his projects which failed to flourish – farming and market-gardening, both of which ventures were speedily reduced in scope, and Tunbridge Wells in particular (his expression would become distinctly vague whenever it was mentioned).

In 1926 Fanny Mounsey and the Thornely Gibsons tried out *Die Entführung* in the Organ Room at Glyndebourne, and 1928 saw the centre of opera switched permanently from Tunbridge Wells to Glyndebourne, with a *Marriage of Figaro* in April in which Christie played the essentially *buffo* part (one in which the singing is of secondary significance) of Antonio the gardener, and then Act III of *Die Meistersinger* on 3 June, with the ubiquitous Thorneley Gibsons as Eva and Hans Sachs, accompanied by a Mrs Lampson at the piano and an equally shadowy Mr Potter on the organ.

Christie's own success as Beckmesser can be gauged by the fact that he spent three hundred hours being coached in the part by Fanny Mounsey. The resulting performance was such, says Blunt, that one of the Glyndebourne housemaids had to be carried out in hysterics.

But clouds were gathering over this Chekhovian idyll. In August the Christie–Mounsey ensemble went back to Munich and Salzburg for more operas, and returned with plans for a revised *Entführung* for the following year. But when the Mounseys descended on Glyndebourne for the 1929 Whitsun weekend, Johnnie Mounsey set off for a walk one day and did not return. His body was found a week later: he had committed suicide in a wood near Redhill.

'He was very fond of Fanny and she in a queer way of him … His death seems to have been the result of a brainstorm resulting from the heat', wrote Christie obliquely to his mother a week later. Fanny and her children moved back to London. Glyndebourne itself was closed down and then let, since Christie felt himself unable to spend a night in the house. He moved into Childs's cottage in Ringmer, and remained there for several months. But if 1929 was John Christie's year of darkness, 1930 was to bring great light.

Not that it started well. On 7 April his father Augustus Christie died. Progressive mental illness, indistinguishable in its symptoms from Alzheimer's Disease, had rendered him generally inarticulate but still able to visit his local club and invite his neighbours to occasional shooting parties, and this in turn had promoted the idea locally that he was a poor old soul very badly treated by an impossible wife.

As the hard-pressed Lady Rosamund had long suspected, he had been secretly helped to make a new Will, in which he left Tapeley and some money not to his wife or his son but to a young cousin, Otho Nicholson. Moreover, not only had this Will been witnessed by two doctors, there had also been another two doctors looking on. In short, it was a Will designed to withstand the most determined assault on its maker's mental capacity. Notwithstanding the strength of feeling against her locally, Lady Rosamund was determined to contest this later Will on the grounds of her husband's lack of testamentary capacity, and within five days of learning its contents had issued a writ to that effect. Lawsuits, then as now, grind slowly, and it was perhaps to take his mind off this and other sorrows that Christie reopened the house at Glyndebourne with the intention of proceeding with the original plan to revive the *Meistersinger* excerpt, to be given at Christmas.

This time the Thornely Gibsons refused to take part, so he

substituted *Entführung* and, on the advice of a Gibson contact, engaged a slim dark soubrette named Audrey Mildmay, a member of the Carl Rosa Opera Company, to sing Blonde for five guineas, more than double her weekly wage with the Carl Rosa company. Few single performances can have had a more lasting effect on opera in Britain. Before Audrey left, Christie had shown her one of the Glyndebourne bedrooms, with the rather daunting introduction, 'This is where we shall sleep when we are married.'

For a man who had remained single until the age of forty-seven, Christie approached the delicate task of wooing the beautiful Miss Mildmay, then aged thirty, with remarkable aplomb if, as the remark noted above seems to indicate, a distinct lack of finesse. Happily, his customary approach to any problem – full frontal assault – proved successful. After six months of being bombarded by letters, often two or more a day, accompanied by hampers of food, fox furs, solid silver roses and every other device available to a lovesick impresario, as she toured the provinces with the Carl Rosa Company singing the lead soprano in *Pagliacci* and *Carmen*, Audrey Mildmay married John Christie on 4 June 1931, with Childs as best man. Only a few weeks before, his mother had won a triumphant victory in the High Court, overturning Augustus Christie's second Will and thus keeping the Tapeley inheritance intact and putting the Nicholsons and their cohorts to flight (and to very considerable personal expense as well).

The honeymoon turned out to be incident-filled rather than romantic, as first Audrey had her appendix out in a German clinic and then, 'to keep her company,' he followed suit. They returned to Glyndebourne on 4 August, and one may surmise that the idea of a more elaborate space for home-grown opera was already very much on Christie's mind. Within a year it had gelled into an extension to the Organ Room large enough to hold a hundred and fifty people, and preliminary trenches for the footings had already been dug.

No one familiar with building works will make the mistake of underestimating the negative impact of footings. These, the concrete bases along which the walls of the rooms will rise, always appear to be far too small for whatever edifice it is planned will sit upon them. Was Audrey Christie affected by this, or by a more far-reaching calculation of what was possible? Whatever the reason, on hearing her husband discussing those particular plans with Hamish Wilson, the stage designer, she interrupted them with the now-famous words: 'If you're going to spend all that money, John, for God's sake do the job properly!'

However varied the myths may be that have arisen around the Christies, all are agreed on one point: this was the moment when what might have been one more amateurish arts venture turned instead into 'the English Salzburg', the standard against which all opera on this island was to be judged over the (to date) next sixty years, and became an irrefutable – and therefore studiously ignored – rebuttal of those who demand increasing State subsidy as the *sine qua non* of quality in grand opera.

At the age of forty-eight, John Christie had at last found the two things he had always lacked: domestic happiness, and a real task in life, one for which his customary vigour and attention to detail made him uniquely well-fitted.

Even so, luck played a helpful role. Hammerstein had fled Germany to escape his father's violence; now others were setting off on the same voyage, though this time the threat was political rather than domestic. By 1932 the rise of Adolf Hitler and his Nazi party, intent on blaming all Germany's misfortunes on its Jewish population, had instigated a small but increasingly noticeable flow of both Jews and dissenting Germans into exile. This was especially the case after the official establishment of the Third Reich in 1933, which precipitated the immediate emigration of artists such as Klemperer, Walter, Schnabel and Busch.

The building at Glyndebourne, now re-sited and planned to

seat three hundred and eleven, progressed quickly, spurred on both by Christie's fear of increased taxation under a Labour Government and by his irrepressible presence in the trenches, up the ladders, even teetering across the scaffolding planks. As his own architect, and with his own building company, there was nothing to hold him back, and his scientific bent was amply tested and fulfilled in devising and perfecting the various electric and theatrical intricacies involved in such an undertaking.

In August 1932 the Christies were in Munich for more operas, and then Audrey went on to Vienna to study with the highly-recommended Jani Strasser while Christie returned to Glyndebourne to continue his supervision of the new theatre.

Part of his success undoubtedly stemmed from his ability to shelve other less absorbing or less successful commitments in order to concentrate single-mindedly on the project that mattered. The organ business, which had actually shown good profits in the late twenties with the rising demand for cinema organs – notably the Christie Unit Organ, which could produce a wide spectrum of effects including 'Sleigh Bells' and 'Crockery Smash' and was priced from £1,145 up to £4,594 for those required to operate in the Tropics – experienced a marked decline once the 'Talkies' had been developed in Hollywood.

It must have been around this time that Christie, meeting Garrett Moore in Brooks's club, remarked that, as he owned an organ-building business, he intended to place a number of keyboards in his orchestra pit, each one linked to a different set of pipes representing the various wind instruments. 'That should keep the running costs down!' he told his politely sceptical companion. Luckily for the ultimate success of Glyndebourne, no conductor was ever asked to accommodate this variation to the more traditional constituents of an orchestra.

In December 1932 Christie went out to Vienna to bring his wife home for Christmas, and casually invited Strasser to come over to Glyndebourne to advise on their project. Strasser clearly thought this was no more than conversational politeness, but in

February 1933 Christie telephoned him indignantly to ask why he still hadn't arrived.

February 1933, with the opera house rising steadily on its enlarged foundations, brought not only the Strassers to Sussex, but also the news that Audrey Christie was expecting a child. A barn was being converted as a restaurant, seats had been ordered, Sir Thomas Beecham was invited to perform (he never troubled to reply) and ninety-five pounds were invested in a 'cloud-apparatus'. Certain that stage lighting was capable of far greater effects than those customarily allowed for on opera stages, Christie immersed himself first in learning about and then in manufacturing himself the apparatus needed to achieve what he wanted.

On 29 June 1933 the first news of Glyndebourne appeared in the *London Evening News*, when the report that a 'Captain Christie' was building an opera-house for his wife to sing in was met with predictable scepticism. What a disservice Oscar Hammerstein and (since 1940) *Citizen Kane* have done to the reputations of singers who marry (or bed) their impresarios (or record-producers). Overnight their talents are forgotten, and every role they gain is seen to be won not from merit but by means of undue influence.

In November 1933 the *Daily Telegraph* noted that the new theatre would be inaugurated with a private performance 'for Mr Christie's friends and tenants'. In short, the general view was still that this was merely a rich man's slightly comic toy.

Christie even wrote again to Thomas Beecham, then very much the Great Panjandrum of British opera and still (thanks to his father's astonishing purchase of the whole Covent Garden estate, including the Royal Opera House, from the Duke of Bedford on the eve of the Great War) part-owner of Covent Garden itself. Old Sir Joseph Beecham, prevented by sudden wartime measures from raising the loan needed to complete his purchase, had watched aghast as this outstanding gesture of support for his mercurial son turned spectacularly sour, the interest on the purchase eventually wiping out the entire fortune he had accumulated from his famous liver pills. As well as indigent owner, Thomas Beecham was more particularly artistic director/conductor to the Covent Garden Board, which was why Christie pressed him to visit Glyndebourne:

(a) in order that my wife should have the pleasure of meeting you;
(b) that you should form an opinion as to the suitability of the Opera House for the Mozart Festspiele which has been planned;
(c) so that we can discuss the advisability of the German and the English Mozart Festspiele at the beginning and the end of June;
(d) so that I can have further personal discussion with you on the Covent Garden plans.

Again, Beecham did not bother to reply.

That November had also brought Adolf Busch, the famous German violinist, to Eastbourne. Staying the night locally, he was taken over to Glyndebourne, and when he was told that the Christies were without a conductor, he suggested his brother Fritz. Until recently Fritz Busch had been the Musical Director of the Dresden Opera, but he had left Germany in protest at the Nazification of the musical profession, despite being offered Toscanini's position at Bayreuth.

Plans for the inaugural 1934 season at first leaned heavily towards Wagner, but feeling that the delicate beauty of Mozart was more suited to a small theatre (and perhaps also to her own voice) than the massive bombast of Wagner, Audrey Christie, strongly supported by their designer Hamish Wilson, pushed for Mozart above Wagner. Fritz Busch, then in Copenhagen, was invited to conduct a 'fortnight's Mozart festival' in June. He refused at first, being contracted to work in Buenos Aires, but when this was cut short he wrote to say that he would come, privately believing this first season at Glyndebourne would also be the last.

Busch met John Christie in Amsterdam (Christie dressed in loosely-fitting tweeds and, in one doubtful version of the encounter, clutching a pug), persuaded him that the right operas to do would be *Così fan tutte* and *Le Nozze di Figaro*, and adamantly over-ruled Christie's lingering thoughts that the accompaniment might be suitably provided by his brother Adolf's Busch String Quartet fortified by a Christie Unit Organ.

Once the role of 'producer' had been explained to him, Christie wrote to Carl Ebert, who had produced *Die Entführung* at Salzburg for Busch the year before and was currently *Generalintendant* of the Charlottenburg Opera in Berlin. Ebert, thinking Christie's letter – about a *private* opera! – to be the work of a lunatic (Beecham was not alone in believing the idea ridiculous), did not reply. A second letter only deepened his conviction. Then Christie sent him a telegram, and out of curiosity Ebert came in February to visit the site.

What he found – there was no fly tower, no scenery dock – was not encouraging, but in countering all his objections Christie stuck to a simple formula: the money side was no one's business but his own, and he would provide. All he wanted to know was whether Ebert would consent to present this inaugural season, together with Busch.

Faced with such stubborn flexibility, Ebert agreed, but subject to one most stringent condition: that, *while they would discuss everything with Christie first*, the final decision on the casting, terms, repertoire and rehearsing would be for Ebert and Busch alone.

For most businessmen, such a demand would have been both morally and psychologically impossible to meet. The struggles associated with reaching absolute power generally preclude any ability to devolve that power irreversibly. But the whole nature of Christie's development – his inheritance, his wartime service, his loyalty to and reliance on his subordinates – made it a small matter to him to accept the deal without demur; for him, perhaps, it was no different from yielding to his head keeper's regime in the woods.

Many similar deals in opera have been made on paper: Christie was unique both in keeping to its terms, even (or, rather, especially) when they were at their most onerous, and in thus creating the framework which was to turn a *jeu d'esprit* into a major international institution.

If the general public had been dubious about Captain Somebody-or-Other building a private opera house, the musical world had been quite as sceptical of Christie's announced plans, which initially were for a preliminary season of *Die Walküre* and *Don Giovanni*, followed by the entire *Ring* and *Parsifal*. The publication of the more plausible programme of *Così* and *Figaro* aroused the first genuine interest in this project. Christie had issued a personal manifesto:

Glyndebourne Opera House has two possibilities:

1. To offer superb performances to people who will regard them as the chief thing in the day or week to be looked forward to, and who will not try to sandwich them between business interviews and a society party.

2. To give educational performances for the ordinary public, with the best possible stage setting and only English orchestras and lesser known singers.

I incline towards the superb performance, assisted by a marvellous '*Festspiel*' atmosphere, but expense would prevent the admission of the poorer portion of the public, and so it may be desirable to give local performances after the '*Festspiel*' is over. ... There are no vested interests, no traditions in the way.

Few pioneering versions can have been so exactly or so enduringly brought to fruition: this template is still being reproduced to the letter sixty years later by John Christie's son and grandchildren (a dynastic similarity with the Wagners that he could hardly have foreseen when first he drove across Europe's dirt roads to Bayreuth in 1911).

Christie himself was busy driving, encouraging and inventing, adapting all sorts of contraptions for use backstage and front-of-house. Although in later life he looked back nostalgically to his years at Eton, it is impossible to believe that he did not revel in the busy and complex chaos that must have now enveloped his otherwise quiet Sussex estate. Ebert had encouraged Rudolf Bing, who had been with him in Charlottenburg, to come over to England and join Alfred Nightingale in dealing with the administration of contracts and general running. Jock Gough, whom Christie had first recruited at the Tunbridge Wells season, was stage foreman and cheerfully bore the brunt of most of Christie's personal interventions.

At last, on Monday, 28 May 1934, the Glyndebourne Festival Opera gave its inaugural performance: Mozart's *Le Nozze di Figaro*, sung in Italian, with Audrey Christie, expecting her second child (their son George Christie was born on 31 December, an event commemorated with a book signed by six hundred of the Christies' tenants and employees), as Susanna. It was a day when the BBC were firmly defending their decision to interrupt a rare broadcast of Act III of *Lohengrin*, live from Beecham's Covent Garden performance, in mid-aria in order to announce the next day's Weather Forecast; the reason given for the interruption was that 'the opera started late'.

It is clear from the programme for this first performance that Christie wished to stress the cosmopolitan element in his cast and at the same time emphasise his employment of British singers. Although the orchestra had to be content with the bald announcement that 'Every Member of the Orchestra and of the Chorus has been personally selected', the cast list detailed each singer's nationality, even to the extent of:

Count   Roy Henderson   (Scotch)

Stalls were two pounds each on the first night, and the wearing of evening dress (white tie) was 'recommended', as was the 3.10 afternoon train from Victoria (ten shillings and sixpence return) for those travelling from London. More than a hundred came, including John Christie's mother, his father-in-law, county neighbours such as the Gages from Firle, the Monk Brettons from Conyboro and the Baxendales from Framfield, and a sprinkling of Bright Young Things like Diana Cooper, Charlotte Bonham-Carter and Cecil Beaton.

No one can have known quite what to expect, but after the more sparsely attended but equally well-prepared *Così fan tutte* the following night, and the very favourable reviews, it was clear that the hard work had been worth while. The combination of an attractive cast, painstaking rehearsal in acting as well as singing, and Busch's meticulous orchestral work gave the performances a gloss of professionalism which overcame the initial suspicions that this was all no more than a rich man's toy. Spike Hughes, then a music critic for the *Daily Herald*, described the effect as 'sensational'.

By 10 June, it was all over. The originating team had given twelve performances in thirteen days, with an average audience of around a hundred, and Christie had lost seven thousand pounds on the fortnight, which was what he had budgeted for. Work began immediately to prepare for the following summer, with *Die Zauberflöte* and *Die Entführung* to be added to the existing repertoire. The provision of a scenery dock, which had been prevented by Christie's temporary refusal to sacrifice a precious ilex tree, was now permitted, while Busch, who now admitted to having accepted the first season in the expectation that there would never be a second, said with affectionate far-sightedness: 'The idyll of 1934 was once upon a time. It will not come again.'

Not even Christie's enthusiastic authority could protect Glyndebourne from the inevitable penalties of success. Recordings were made; singers demanded vastly increased fees (a mere Pedrillo was now asking eighty pounds a show, as compared to the first Belmonte, who had accepted twenty-four; Pamina got fourteen!); the administrators, Nightingale and Bing, fell down badly on securing written contracts for the new casts; Audrey Christie first could not, and then could, be available to sing Pamina, thus further upsetting the chaotic casting arrangements which drove Busch to threaten resignation on 18 April 1935.

Writing to Bing to reprove him for allowing Souez (his Fiordiligi) to commit herself to Beecham at Covent Garden, Busch said,

> You must know that 'bad behaviour' is the *rule* among singers. ... I *demand* that the five guilty ones [they included John Christie] do *everything* with, without or against Beecham, with the help of the King, or Parliament, of friend or foe, no matter HOW: that I have Souez at the necessary rehearsals and the 4–5 performances of *Così*. Where there's a will, there *is* a way ... This IS possible. That is my last word.

In fact, negotiations with Beecham were made far more difficult than they need have been because of Christie's overwhelming confidence in his own product, which led him to express his opinion of other people's with a breathtaking want of tact.

Julius Harrison, Musical Director of the Hastings Municipal Band, had written to Christie to ask for some free seats. This had unleashed a diatribe from Christie on the poor standard of music in England, *particularly* at Covent Garden. Harrison disobligingly managed to embroil Beecham in the correspondence, and he wrote back to Harrison:

> I have had ample opportunity of hearing the tests made ... at the first Glyndebourne Festival, and if these be fair samples of the general results obtained there then I more than agree with you that in the important matters of execution, style and accuracy in the interpretation of Mozart we have not only nothing to learn but a great deal to teach!

Harrison helpfully forwarded this letter to Christie, thus ensuring maximum offence all round.

Nevertheless, negotiations were somehow completed successfully, and both Souez and Busch were in their respective places when the 1935 Season got under way.

The *Zauberflöte* was a further revelation of the benefits of thorough preparation and fine casting, despite a disappointing Queen of the Night who then also had to be dumped from *Entführung*; Noël Eadie took over as Constanze, a role entirely new to her, at a few days' notice, in a crisis more redolent of Mapleson than of Glyndebourne. Childs the butler, however, was a smash hit in the silent role of Der Stumme, on a standard contract at a fee of fifteen guineas for the season.

This second season produced a loss of ten thousand pounds, despite slowly increasing audiences and the sale, to those dining in the interval, of nearly a thousand bottles from Christie's extensive list of fine German wines, a vast increase over 1934. A major part of the charm of Glyndebourne was (and still is) its relaxed attitude to dinner. From the start the audience were encouraged to stroll through and picnic in the extensive gardens, with (this being England) the wise alternative available of restaurant service under cover. Just as Hammerstein had learnt from Koster and Bial that the catering profits from entertainment were potentially a major consideration in the budget, so Christie, perhaps unintentionally, found that the sale of food and of his German wine was already helping to defray his operational costs.

It was promptly announced that the 1936 Season would run to thirty-five performances. *Don Giovanni* (with Audrey Christie as Zerlina) was added, to make a total of five Mozart operas. A subscription ticket could be bought for thirteen pounds five shillings, which included a ten-shilling dinner on each of five chosen evenings, and there was even a system of Christmas Ticket Vouchers. Nightingale left, to be replaced by Bing as General Manager. The original acoustics had not been a success, so a major refit was carried out which included the provision of an illuminated path from the car park, a new dining hall, and extensive work on the stage and auditorium.

This period between 1932 and 1936 was John Christie's creative zenith. These were the years when, in his early fifties, he envisaged, created and brought to triumphant fruition, in his own family home, what became and has remained one of the three major opera festivals of the world, with Salzburg and Bayreuth.

Spike Hughes, author of the definitive history of Glyndebourne, makes the interesting point that, although opera was actually started as a private entertainment in a private house (in the city of Florence), it had, after the 1637 inauguration of the Teatro San Cassiano in Venice, become an essentially urban as well as public entertainment. (In saying this, he presumably discounted the many operas Haydn wrote and presented at Eszterhaza, the relatively rustic seat of his patron Prince Esterhazy.) By taking opera into the countryside, Christie had therefore attempted (and eventually achieved) something revolutionary.

This magnificently ironical result, whereby a schoolmaster, an amateur in music, brought off something that generations of financiers and professional impresarios had tried for and failed, should not be overshadowed by what was to be a long subsequent period of unexceptional twilight.

Christie was a fine employer, and a devoted family man. But he had an Achilles heel which was to dog his later years with persistent discomfort: his sense of proportion, always an unsteady possession in men surrounded exclusively by their own employees, began to let him down.

As early as March 1936 John Christie made a speech in which he publicly announced that 'If any English composer is prepared to write an opera which the staff of Glyndebourne consider really good, we shall be prepared to put it on.' He went further: he wrote letters to *The Times* and to other newspapers, reiterating the offer, and reflecting on the 'inevitable failure' of earlier English offerings, restricted as they had been to being produced under 'scratch conditions'.

Even well-disposed musicians took against these condescending words. To his old enemy Julius Harrison (of the Hastings Municipal Band) they offered the perfect excuse for a further outpouring of bile:

> The organization at Glyndebourne is essentially *German*. Mr Christie models his whole scheme on Munich and Salzburg, and glories in it ... but if he imagines that British composers are going to rush in to submit their operas to his very *un-British* musical staff, he is in for disillusionment ...

Busch, Ebert, Strasser and Bing, refugees from similar sentiments in Germany, must have felt this tone to be horribly familiar.

Moreover, the failing which had marred Christie's effectiveness as a teacher – a real difficulty in passing on to those listening a complex point which seemed quite obvious to himself – resurfaced in his didactic certainty of Glyndebourne's superiority, and in his trenchant disdain for every other company's work. Meeting the director after a particularly successful Sadler's Wells performance, he congratulated him: 'Well, that was very good; very good indeed. You really must come to Glyndebourne, and do it *for the tenants*.' A master of this kind of unintentional sting, he wrote back to one aspiring applicant: 'If you can sing above average, and act as well as you can sing, and are tall and reasonably good-looking, we could give you an audition *for our chorus*.' He warned another singer in advance that he wanted 'no screechers' at Glyndebourne.

When Audrey Christie wrote to him from Rome, where she was studying to improve her Italian, 'Don't hammer your points unduly. You carry enough wait (*sic*) now to put your stuff across softly and easily!!!', and again, 'You have your stuff so clear in your own mind that you don't make it clear to others', she was, unconsciously, echoing the very points made so long ago by his Eton colleagues. Moran Caplat was later to describe him as being often right, *but for the wrong reason.*

Although the 1936 deficit fell to four thousand pounds, helped by a broadcasting contract with the BBC and the sale of two and a half thousand bottles of wine to dining audiences, the preparations for 1937 produced the first major rift between Christie and his *quattuorvirate.* As he grew in confidence in his own musical judgement, so he wished, understandably, to have more say in the casting. This Busch and Ebert resisted, and even sent him a firmly worded letter from Bing, reminding him of his earlier undertaking to them both.

Christie wrote back accepting the point, and ending his letter: 'Best wishes and love from Glyndebourne to you and your family, The dog is well, yours ever'. . . .

In 1937 the auditorium, now widened by Christie's own Ringmer Building Works, held four hundred and thirty-three seats. The same five productions were given, and Glyndebourne produced its first profit: nearly three thousand pounds, and a source of great satisfaction.

In March 1938 they nearly lost Bing. He was caught inside Austria on the 12th when Hitler invaded, and only his chance possession of a special passport (borrowed from an MP) allowed him to escape what would have led him, as a Jew, to the concentration camps.

That season, under the usual operatic imperative of new works needing to be brought in to retain customer loyalty, Busch accepted the Christies' candidate, Donizetti's *Don Pasquale,* in return for adding his own choice, Verdi's *Macbeth.* One sign of Busch's eminence was that Toscanini and Furtwängler both came to see the *Macbeth.* They chose the same night, however, which was unfortunate since they were seriously at odds over how best to deal with the Nazi menace. Four thousand bottles of wine were sold and drunk that year, but the

Festival had slipped back into deficit, losing seven thousand pounds.

On a different front, Christie had become official adviser to King George VI on buying German wines. Here too his approach was idiosyncratic, as can be seen from a surviving letter to Buckingham Palace:

Dear Sir,

I cannot read your signature and, of course, I ought to know who is Financial Secretary. My impression is that it was Adeane, but I can see a dot over your signature, which makes it impossible. [The name was Adeane; possibly the dot arose from his Christian name, Michael.] ... I find that German wines do not taste equally well in all places. Glyndebourne seems to be good; Tapeley is bad. ... It is therefore conceivable that Balmoral or Sandringham might be fortunate. I suppose one can only find this out by trial. Red wines are good at Tapeley. It is one of those queer things ...

Satisfied with what was being achieved at Glyndebourne, Christie now began to turn his eye to a scheme for managing Covent Garden in tandem with his own Festival, and wrote: 'I suppose it depends on whether Beecham makes a muddle and a loss again this year. This is in confidence, but I want Covent Garden to be combined with us ...' He added more seats to Glyndebourne now, and enlarged the stage.

For all Christie's plans to take over Covent Garden, Beecham was not above a little scheming himself. He offered Bing the job of General Manager at the Royal Opera House, suggesting it was a role he could combine with his work at Glyndebourne, and this move possibly contained the germ of a reverse-takeover. Bing refused, and Glyndebourne itself received touring offers from Switzerland and New York.

However, as the plans advanced to repeat the previous year's operas between 1 June and 15 July 1939, the very phenomenon that had made Glyndebourne's success possible was preparing to snatch it away. What might have been no more than a light-weight, evanescent rustic idyll had been given gravitas and status by the flight from Germany and Austria of a number of highly talented artists, while without the Nazis' oppression of the Jews, none of the *quattuorviri* would ever have dreamt of side-lining themselves from the mainstream Continental opera world amid the quiet Sussex Downs. But now war was inescapably in the air.

On 27 September 1938 the Glyndebourne London office was evacuated to Sussex. The following day, the British fleet was mobilised. On 29 September, Chamberlain signed away Czechoslovakia at Munich. 'Peace in our time'? The Glyndebourne Germans were sceptical, but on 15 October a general meeting decided to proceed with plans for the 1939 Festival, though with the exercise of maximum economy. In January 1939 Bing and Ebert crossed to New York to try to arrange for a Glyndebourne expedition to the World Fair there in August.

A long-running source of discord among the Festival's principals – the Christies' persistence in continuing to travel to Germany – was made much worse at this time when Audrey Christie accepted offers to sing in Berlin in the spring and again at the Salzburg Festival in August. The invitations were of course a great honour musically, but severely tainted by their political overtones.

'She would not just metaphorically but literally be shaking hands with murderers,' wrote Bing in an agonised appeal to Busch to intercede.

Despite the ill-feeling their actions aroused, the Christies did travel to Hamburg, and Audrey Christie sang at concerts there and in Berlin. However, even the Permanent Secretary at the Foreign Office, when asked by Christie to support his wife's

Salzburg plan, wrote back to say that *on balance* he advised against it. Faced with such general opposition, she cancelled. It must have been a very grave disappointment.

In April a scratch team which included Audrey Christie, Ina Souez and Busch performed *Figaro* and *Don Giovanni* in Brussels and Antwerp, with Glyndebourne costumes and borrowed sets. Back home, the theatre had been altered to fit in five hundred and thirty-seven seats, and the Festival had been extended: it was now to run from 1 June until Saturday 15 July, with a new record of thirty-eight performances.

On the last night Christie appeared on stage to announce 'serious news'. Given the constantly changing political situation, and Hitler's penchant for weekend coups, it must have been a relief to some of the audience at least when they learned the news was that Harrow had defeated Eton at cricket for the first time in thirty-two years. The next day it was announced that the 1940 Festival would include *Carmen*, *Figaro*, *Macbeth*, *Don Giovanni* and *Zauberflöte*. Within two months, however, Britain was at war, and two hundred and sixty evacuated London children had been billeted at Glyndebourne.

The war scattered Glyndebourne's cast: Busch went to South America, Ebert to Turkey, and Audrey Christie and her two children to Canada, for their safety. Bing got a job in the Peter Jones department store in Sloane Square, and Christie himself, too old now to fight, retired to Tapeley where, lonely and approaching sixty, he became increasingly determined to make use of his energies in setting up some form of national operatic body. His first idea was a National Council of Music, through which he would cure 'the bungling amateur approach to musical performance in England'. Correspondence flowed, and not all of it one way, or signed:

Where are your GERMAN opera directors now? Behind barbed wire we hope. But you must find some more if you can. Don't encourage your own country in art – always have

Germans – mediocrities or Italians. What you want is a GERMAN BOMB under you to knock some sense into you. Not to spend your *UNEARNED* Dividends with the GERMANS.

Childs the butler died that autumn. Christie wrote to his son George:

I am so sorry about Childs. He was with me for about 30 years. He died peacefully in Lewes hospital. He was cremated and a bunch of roses from you, with the inscription 'from his loving godson George', was placed in front of the earn [*sic*]. I know you were fond of him. I was. And he adored both you and me. He was a witty man and a very good man. I hope you will try to remember Childs with respect and affection. In your work and doings try to be as good a man as he was …

With Glyndebourne now effectively a kindergarten, Christie spent most of his time at Tapeley, where the house had been turned into a guest house. Oddly, Margaret Belshaw, who worked at the Estate Office there, reported later that:

He spent a good deal of time digging into family history. He talked incessantly of his early life. I gathered that at one time there had been a strong bond between him and his father. Of his mother he was always critical, although often, after talking about her, he would add, 'My mother was a good woman.'

There is no other evidence of anything except a most troubled and distant relationship between him and his father. It is almost as though he were blaming himself for his father's manifest shortcomings, and indulging in a nostalgic rearranging of the true state of his childhood. If so, it was a most uncharacteristic

attack of wistful fantasy in an otherwise trenchantly straightfor-
ward man.

In many families, troubled relations between the generations
have a habit of repeating themselves. Not so with Christie. His
son George, writing in 1997, records: '[My father] was an extra-
ordinarily benign parent possessing huge generosity towards his
family,' adding: 'his boundless eccentricity was acutely embar-
rassing to me when I was about ten. There was a considerable
generation gap – more like a double generation – but I was
never conscious of this, which speaks rather well of him.'

Meanwhile in Canada, and later in New York, Audrey
Christie and the children were leading a very difficult existence.
She had little money, as it was not allowed to be transferred from
England, and often no heating. One English personage she
came across was Beecham, who spent the war years moving
profitably around America and Australia. Indeed, he even
engineered her last stage performance, as Susanna in Montreal.
He took the trouble of sending John Christie a telegram:

HAVE JUST CONDUCTED TWO PERFORMANCES MOSTLY WITH MET-
ROPOLITAN SINGERS OF MOZARTS FIGARO FOR MONTREAL FESTI-
VAL IN WHICH AUDREY AS SUSANNA HAS SCORED A BRILLIANT AND
SPECIAL SUCCESS WHICH I THINK WILL HAVE FORTUNATE RESULTS
– BEECHAM.

But he was also reported as having described Audrey as 'a nice
little woman married to an awful fool of a husband'.

This might well have been the view increasingly held in
official circles, as Christie bombarded those in authority with
letters about the inadequacy of everything musical other than
Glyndebourne: 'I am not satisfied with much of the musical side
of the BBC's work – good music and rubbish. ... It seems to me
you want a Director of a Committee of Cultural
Reconstruction ...' He badgered R. A. Butler, then Minister for
education; Anthony Eden at the Foreign Office; the Prime

Minister; the Director-General of the BBC. To the Minister of Aircraft Production he wrote: 'I have several problems which perhaps may interest you, because they concern the building of the New World in the matter of the mind and the spirit. First, the Future of Glyndebourne ...' Most of these letters received the barest acknowledgement.

Another plan was for twenty thousand people to invest ten pounds each in a Glyndebourne Society. He wanted the Members of the Cabinet to join first, followed by the Press, Clergy, Lawyers ... and Learned Societies: 'It's a grand scheme ... one million members ...' It seems that their sixties are difficult years for opera impresarios.

To Audrey, who was sent copies of all these initiatives, he wrote: 'I am taking note of your suggestions about blowing my own trumpet. I am not arrogant or conceited, but I know Glyndebourne has been a marvel and it seems silly to pretend otherwise ...' Without a doubt she was Christie's very best friend, able to warn him frankly of his excesses from a position of unquestioned love. But he took very little notice. There are some professions which tend to lead to an impervious disregard of conventional criticism: being a judge is one, being a schoolmaster is another. The characteristic which had helped him override conventional hurdles in creating Glyndebourne now prevented him from maintaining the personal prestige which might have enabled him to play a greater part in the post-war national scene.

Audrey and he were reunited in 1944 when the family returned to England, ironically just in time for the V-2 rockets which posed the only real danger to Glyndebourne throughout the war. An unexpected bonus was that the war had brought prosperity to Christie's businesses as it had to many others. In 1944 his direct income from his various concerns was not much less than fifty thousand pounds (perhaps half the total cost of building and running the opera between 1932 and 1939), with the Ringmer Building Works contributing fourteen thousand of this. No matter that taxation took most of what he drew as income: it was profit, and therefore available to be reinvested for the future.

As the war drew to a close, one pressing uncertainty was the future of the Royal Opera House. It was currently rented to Mecca Cafés, who had run it throughout the war as a highly profitable tea-house and wished to continue with their lease, the terms of which gave them protection in every way but one: it could be broken by the presentation of grand opera.

The present building had been re-erected by Edward Barry in 1856, after a fire – fires being a usual hazard in the days of candles on stage and gas-lights in the auditorium. Built on land owned by the Dukes of Bedford, the theatre had been consistently leased out (at around seven thousand pounds a year) for opera, whether to individuals like Ernest Gye and Thomas Beecham (who presented the first night of *Rosenkavalier* there), or to syndicates like that headed by Augustus Harris. It was then bought by Beecham's father Joseph in 1914, inherited by Beecham, and subsequently sold by him in 1924 to a public company, Covent Garden Estates Limited, in which he had a large shareholding. It had since been managed by a syndicate, with Beecham as artistic director, which since 1931 had been regularly receiving around twenty-five thousand pounds a year from the BBC in return for broadcasting rights. In 1939 Beecham's mistress, Emerald Cunard, effectively underwrote the last opera season there before the war. It included performances of *Der Ring* with Germaine Lubin and Lauritz Melchior, *Aïda* with Beniamino Gigli and Eva Turner, *Turandot* with Turner again and Giovanni Martinelli, and *Don Giovanni* with Ezio Pinza, Elisabeth Rethberg and Richard Tauber. It was to be many years before such a standard was reached again.

Two other factors proved relevant to the fate of the Royal Opera House after the Second World War. John Maynard Keynes, who from their schooldays at Eton had nursed a deep dislike for Christie, was becoming influential in a number of fields, in particular as first Chairman of the Arts Council of Great Britain. This was originally a private initiative, largely funded from the United States by the Pilgrim Trust, but had been taken over by the Board of Education and was now wholly funded by the Treasury.

Secondly, the post-war years rapidly became the Age of Corporate Committee Man, and while Keynes was at his best in a committee, it would be hard to imagine anyone less likely to shine in such a setting than Christie. He and Beecham were both relics of a more self-reliant age, whereas 1945 was to herald a four-year surge of State nationalisation during which such entities as the Ringmer & District Electricity Co., the coal mines, the steel industry – and soon, rather improbably, the Royal Opera House – would fall under government control. The new hands on the levers of State believed in corporate rather than individual power.

Both Christie and Beecham had their own plans to acquire Covent Garden, and both were as mortified and as deeply aggrieved as were Mecca Cafés when a new Covent Garden Trust took over the lease through Boosey and Hawkes, the music publishers, and appointed David Webster, a Liverpool draper, as General Manager. Sir Kenneth Clark wanted Christie at least to be included on the Board, but the combined coterie of Keynes, the tenor-cum-administrator Steuart Wilson, Webster himself and Edward Dent, the fanatical opera-must-be-sung-in-English translator, defeated him.

Mecca Cafés sued (unsuccessfully), and Beecham, typically blunt, didn't shrink from pointing out the salient characteristic of the new Covent Garden team. To practise homosexuality was still an imprisonable offence in 1945, and his widely-canvassed criticisms must have caused great alarm among certain of the Board members. Years later Beecham remarked that, passing Covent Garden, 'I saw, to my great surprise, that they were actually announcing "The Twilight of the Sods". It's about time.'

Nevertheless, the new Labour Government eventually placed a compulsory purchase order on the Royal Opera House, and it passed out of the world of private enterprise and into a new place among the growing ranks of nationalised and state-subsidised enterprises, where it still remains.

Christie always maintained that he had reached an agreement on the matter, but Lesley Boosey, one of the original Board, remembered it differently. At lunch at Brooks's, Christie told Boosey that he was also in the market for Covent Garden.

I therefore went across the road to the office in King Street, and asked Mr Goddard [of Goddard & Smith, who acted for Covent Garden Properties Ltd] point blank whether Covent Garden was for sale, as Mr Christie had said he was negotiating to buy. Mr Goddard said there was absolutely no question of their selling Covent Garden to JC or anyone else. I therefore believed JC was 'shooting a line' as they say in the Navy ... JC has suggested on various occasions that he agreed to withdraw on the understanding that he should be on the new Board. This is a figment of his imagination. No such arrangement was ever discussed let alone made. All the same I did try to get JC on the Board, but Keynes flatly refused and there was nothing more I could do about it.

Meanwhile, at Glyndebourne the old team was reassembling. Strasser had returned, Ebert was back from Turkey, and Bing from Sloane Square. Busch, who had offended both Ebert over a production credit and (more seriously) the Christies when he did not use Audrey in a wartime *Figaro* in New York, remained away until 1950 (by which time Bing had left), but essentially the pre-war status quo was gradually being recreated.

All sorts of ideas were discussed, including a joint effort with Beecham, which predictably foundered almost immediately, and a similar plan with Jay Pomeroy, an independent impresario operating out of Hammerstein's old theatre on Kingsway, whose subsequent opera losses quickly drove him from the business.

Instead, 12 July 1946 found Benjamin Britten's English Opera Group giving the first night of his *Rape of Lucretia*. This surprising development had come about when Eric Crozier, a close associate of Britten's and the original producer of *Peter Grimes*, met Bing at the Lyric Theatre, Hammersmith in November 1945, and raised the possibility of some form of co-operation. A visit to Glyndebourne led to the setting up of the Glyndebourne English Opera Company with four directors – Christie, Bing, Britten and Crozier – and the Britten entourage motored down in his newly purchased Rolls-Royce on 10 June 1946, settled into the house and prepared for five weeks of rehearsal at Christie's expense.

It was a complete mismatch from the start, as Christie could not see the point of Britten's music, and Britten loathed Christie's squirearchical manner – although, being the better used to concealment, he covered this up except among his close friends, who watched the two men with appalled fascination.

Nor were the other members of the two organisations at peace. Christie himself was probably too generous, and too busy with new ideas, to consider the marked contrast between his own voluntary and distinguished service in the First World War and the way Britten had scurried off to California to sit out the Second World War in comfortable safety, but others were more critical. Moran Caplat, Bing's new assistant, recruited straight from the Navy because his uncle had been estate manager at Glyndebourne, describes Britten as 'a remote withdrawn figure who obviously did not see eye-to-eye with John Christie'.

Bing, who on 6 May, early on in the proceedings, had written to Audrey Christie that *Lucretia* was 'brilliant, full of inspiration and, for John's benefit, full of some lovely tunes', was by October, when they were all on tour in Holland, writing of 'the incredibly unfriendly attitude of the Group' (as the Britten ensemble was known), caused, he felt, by the way in which he stood up to them in the interests of Glyndebourne. The whole project cost Christie twelve thousand pounds, of which three thousand had been put up against loss by the Arts Council. No loss could have been incurred in a less enjoyable cause: even the audiences were distinctly less than enthused.

Britten himself would have preferred to cut the connection with Glyndebourne, and wrote formally asking to purchase the Glyndebourne production of *Lucretia*, at the same time asking Audrey Christie to be a Trustee of his proposed independent company. But the total financial failure of his tour, and his lack of any other source of all-important cash, led to a further, even more at-arms-length (not to say downright hostile) arrangement covering a second new presentation, of *Albert Herring* in 1947. No one was surprised when Christie, greeting the audience on its first night, told them, by way of introduction: 'This isn't *our* kind of thing, you know.'

There was great relief all round when Crozier wrote to tell Bing that they would not be seeking further involvement in 1948 (though this was not before they had tried to bribe Caplat away from Glyndebourne), and indeed proposed to set up their own Festival at Aldeburgh.

Glyndebourne's only production for 1947 had been Gluck's *Orfeo*, with Kathleen Ferrier, stronger in its singing than in its *mise-en-scène*, and with a ballet universally condemned as 'deplorable'. However, a separate initiative that year, in Edinburgh, led to a subsidised tour there, one which effectively inaugurated the Edinburgh Festival, which has continued ever since. But preparations leading up to that August booking were precarious. Georg Szell, the great Hungarian conductor, had, in Busch's continuing absence, agreed to conduct *Figaro* and *Macbeth* for Edinburgh. On arriving for the rehearsals, he took an immediate dislike to the Susanna, who didn't know her part, and insisted on her dismissal. When the Macduff was adjudged equally inadequate, Bing found that Szell had simply packed and left. The tour survived, but such an alarm showed that Glyndebourne had still not recovered its pre-war poise.

In November Christie travelled to New York, pursuing again the prospect of an American base where Glyndebourne productions could be presented, this with a view both to expanding the clientele and to spreading the growing cost of productions. In twenty-four hours he visited New York, Boston and Chicago. Audrey Christie had spent enough time in New York during the war to be able to give him excellent advice: 'Be successful – be happy – don't talk too much, and whatever you do don't let them think you are unwanted in Britain or no one will want you!'

He was far from unwanted in Britain, at any rate in Sussex, but elsewhere neither his advice on how to run Covent Garden nor his general views on taxation had found any sort of answering echo among those in power, and to that extent he may well have felt himself increasingly isolated, and also frustrated because he still considered that he had much to offer. We have a description of Christie at this time, from Edward Dent, as having the 'powdery pink and white surface of a Raeburn, and looking so Victorian that you almost think he's got mutton-chop whiskers.'

The trip to the United States ended inconclusively, and he returned with no prospects of opera, not in America, not even at Glyndebourne. The cause may have been the austerity imposed by the Labour Government, or it may have been his treatment at the combined hands of Covent Garden and Britten, or a combination of the two; whatever the reason, he seemed suddenly, though he remained a very rich man indeed, to have lost his taste for the risk of investing in opera. The 1947 deficit had been eight thousand pounds; in Edinburgh, where the cost was being shouldered by the newly-formed Edinburgh Festival Society, the loss had been nine and a half thousand, and Glyndebourne had been invited back for 1948.

Christie went back to America in May 1948, charmed by the

generous hospitality he met with and by the flattering interest with which his views were received. This time his wife must have expected some sort of positive result, after receiving a cabled request that she should meet the boat with the largest lorry she could find. In fact he came back with no bookings, but with a sixty-pound keg of honey and a ton of sugar and rice (to assuage the acute shortages of strict post-war rationing), which he per-suaded his fellow-passengers to help him smuggle through the Customs in a great variety of bags.

There had been a reconciliation with Beecham, who brought his Royal Philharmonic Orchestra down for some Mozart con-certs; the papers made much of a plan for Christie himself to play the hurdy-gurdy part in a Haydn *divertimento*; Reuters announced a definite three-week engagement at Princeton, though this was later cancelled. Finally Bing, who had been much involved in the American initiative, suddenly announced that he was jumping ship, to become *intendant* of the Met. in New York. This was a severe blow to morale, and it must have seemed that the Glyndebourne idyll was dead, even if the corpse was taking a long time to stop twitching.

Moran Caplat took over as General Manager, and at the same time managed to heal the rift with Busch. The Glyndebourne team returned to Edinburgh with Verdi's *Un Ballo in Maschera* and Mozart's *Così fan tutte*, and Glyndebourne was offered a twenty-five-thousand-pound Festival of Britain State subsidy (not from the Arts Council, but direct from the Treasury) for presenting four Mozart operas in 1951. Out of negotiations stimulated by this, John Spedan Lewis, Bing's erst-while employer at Peter Jones, offered a further twelve and a half thousand pounds towards the 1950 season. Glyndebourne was back in business.

These offers of financial support gave new confidence to the disheartened impresario, and he set about organising the new 1951 season, which was to comprise three weeks in July of alter-nate *Entführung* and *Così fan tutte*, with Sena Jurinac as Fiordiligi, tickets at two guineas, and a new total of five hundred and ninety-two seats in the theatre.

Christie himself was in bad health at this time. In October he had to have his (already useless) left eye removed, and shortly afterwards he suffered a mild heart attack at Victoria Station. Although he recovered from this, he soon had further reason for concern. Audrey Christie had not been in completely good health since her return from America in 1944, and it was now clear that she was seriously ill. She was in hospital in May, during the run-up to the 1951 season. He wrote to her often:

> I was running to hide from Sock [his dog] this evening and turned into the Gents' place in the house. My feet shot away from me and I fell, but with one hand caught hold of the door architrave and with the other held my spectacles (unbent) ... – not bad. Darling I miss you very much ...

The Festival continued under its own steam: *Idomeneo*, conducted by Busch, produced by Ebert, with singers coached by Strasser, plus *Figaro*, *Don Giovanni*, and *Così fan tutte*, fully televised for the first time. Then, in September, Fritz Busch died in the Savoy Hotel.

The Edinburgh excursion paid an unexpected extra dividend. The costs of the 1952 season were substantially defrayed by the new Festival Programme Book, a suggestion of the industrialist Sir Miki Sekers, a Hungarian philanthropist based in Cumberland who had seen and enjoyed Glyndebourne's performances in Edinburgh, and wanted to help. Moreover, the programme advertising arrangements spawned the Glyndebourne Festival Society, a private sponsorship scheme which immediately attracted eight hundred members. Christie's deficit this year had grown to nearly eighteen thousand pounds, although this was reduced by three thousand two hundred pounds from the Society and nearly five thousand from the Programme's advertisers.

Christie himself had for some time been contemplating the setting up of a Trust which would take over Glyndebourne, an idea resisted by Audrey Christie as she feared that it would seriously erode her son George's inheritance. Looked at from one point of view, the opera could be seen as a monstrous growth that threatened to destroy the charm and continuity of their family home – the very features that had given it birth. Writing to Sekers, who supported the Trust idea but also appreciated her misgivings, she said:

> I feel you have expressed a very clear understanding of my point of view when you compare our hopes for Glyndebourne ... with what the Wagner family created ... Personally I only want to know that Glyndebourne may continue in its best form as long as there is any need for it, and that, if George is capable of improving on what we have started, his initiative may not be frustrated or hampered ...

Her reservations were percipient, as similar arrangements, for example those made by some families with the National Trust, came in time to prove deeply unhappy for donors' heirs. The Trust for Glyndebourne was indeed set up, but in an altered form in line with her concerns, so that it protected the family's long-term position.

On 31 May 1953, Audrey Christie died at Glyndebourne. She was just fifty-two years old, and John Christie, who had been still a bachelor at forty-nine, found himself a seventy-one-year-old widower. It was a blow from which he did not recover. He lived on for another nine years, however, spending his time peacefully at Glyndebourne, interested but not obsessively so in the continued prosperity of what he had started.

In 1954 Christie was made a Companion of Honour. As with his proposed Distinguished Service Order in 1916, he tried first to avoid it, and then to divert it to a posthumous award to his wife. When this proposal was refused, he accepted the honour as being a tribute, in his eyes, to her. Later the same year both he and (posthumously) Audrey were awarded the Mozart Medal of the Vienna Mozart Society, a unique recognition of what they had achieved. In 1955 he received an Honorary Degree of Doctor of Music from Oxford University.

Christie's work was done. The Festival was established, and his son George was firmly in place as master of Glyndebourne and Tapeley. He had assumed the Chairmanship of the Festival in 1958, shortly after his marriage to Mary Nicholson (whose surname gave John Christie a moment's unease when first he heard it, lest she should prove to be related to the Tapeley litigants).

He made occasional forays abroad, that year staying with Gladwyn and Cynthia Jebb (her parents had rented Glyndebourne from him after Johnnie Mounsey's suicide) in the British Embassy in Paris when Glyndebourne was performing *Le Comte Ory* at the Théâtre Sarah Bernhardt. Warned that he liked porridge, Lady Jebb went to enormous trouble to provide it, falling back at length on having some prepared and delivered from the NAAFI at the British Army base outside Paris. Delighted by her own ingenuity, she waited to enjoy his satisfaction, only to hear him ordering a croissant instead. In her diary, she records him as an eccentric guest.

When he left, a key was found tied to an old handkerchief, right at the back of a drawer in his bedroom. It turned out to be the most precious key of the safe at Glyndebourne, too precious to be entrusted to anybody at home.

In 1959 Ebert retired, leaving only Strasser of the original *quattuorvirate* still *en poste*. After a magnificent performance of *Rosenkavalier*, John Christie came on stage to present Ebert with a silver rose-bowl. In a speech lasting nearly half an hour he reflected at length on their old sparring partners, Covent

Garden and the Arts Council, but remained entirely silent on the subject of Ebert and his rose-bowl.

He continued to write angry letters to *The Times*, and to any other suitable recipient. His eldest grandson, Hector, was born in 1961, and as a grandfather he took particular pleasure in watching over the baby, even though his other eye was now failing and he could scarcely see. He talked always of Eton now, a place and an institution which continued to hold a major part of his affections after more than forty years of absence. It is sobering to consider that if he had been given a House there, the Glyndebourne phenomenon would never have happened.

On 4 July 1962 John Christie died, at the age of seventy-nine. The following night the audience stood, their heads bowed, in his memory.

His obituary in *The Times* described him as an 'implacable perfectionist' who could seem 'unreasonable'. This, it explained, was because, for Christie, 'reason' smacked of compromise. In retrospect, Christie can be seen as opera's supreme team captain. Where Hammerstein and Mapleson propelled their work forward by sheer professional doggedness, Christie selected his team and then (sometimes reluctantly) stood back and let them work, his own role being triumphantly to provide the stimulus, the resources and the setting for their individual talents. It is remarkable that he alone, the least musically adept of these three titans, created a viable, indeed a triumphantly successful and enduring musical institution.

Each of the three men had to swallow his share of ridicule, but the image of the superannuated army captain putting on some tinpot village enterprise to appease his wife is one it would have been exceptionally hard for Christie to bear, had he ever paid the slightest attention to it.

There is such a massive accumulation of individual failures in every field of opera, where so many disappointed people compete for so many unreachable goals, that it is understandable if their frustrations should fuel a matching appetite for malice. The training John Christie acquired through the sorrows of his parents, the loneliness of boarding school and the sordid horrors of the trenches gave him the ideal rhinocerine nonchalance with which to force his way forward through such a comparatively trivial undergrowth of unpleasantness.

Significantly, when John Christie died he was celebrated locally in Sussex, not for his operas, but as a good neighbour who laboured to provide employment for local families in a time of national hardship.

5

A Summing-up

THE CAREERS OF these three men illustrate the move of opera from the barn-storming alarums of the old-style democratic music-hall-type presentations of Mapleson, where the entertainment value of the evening to the crowd was paramount, through the transition which began during Hammerstein's day, when the *art* of music-making and singing was beginning to take precedence over the spectacle. This was accompanied by a consequent shift in the source of income from the crowd towards a more sedate (and secure) oligarchic financing from private individuals, a route to which Hammerstein found himself unable to adapt. John Christie, of course, completed this move with his essentially monarchic formula, whereby the excellence of the music takes precedence over all monetary considerations. That this latter should have proved the most successful regime financially is one of the ironies of operatic history.

In her excellent book on the history of Covent Garden, Frances Donaldson cites six characteristics supposedly essential for a successful career as an impresario:

1. Energy.
2. Stubbornness.
3. Optimism.
4. Attention to detail.
5. *Terribilità*.
6. Team leadership.

Mapleson surely scores highest for optimism. In his speech at the lunch following the ceremonial laying of the foundation stone for his English National Opera House, he said: 'Before taking any step in this enterprise, I have felt myself bound to be provided with sufficient resources for carrying it through …': within four months the whole scheme had completely collapsed.

Behind his persiflage undoubtedly lay a skilled and resourceful musical mind, and he must also be permitted to score points for team leadership. He could scarcely have undertaken his relentless travelling in the pursuit of success without a fine reserve of energy.

What Mapleson seriously lacked was both the attention to contractural detail which is a prerequisite of sustained commercial success, and *terribilità*; this proved a grave drawback in his business dealings and, in combination with his perhaps excessive optimism, led ultimately to his ruin.

Hammerstein scores very highly for stubbornness and energy. His optimism, too, was boundless, and he had a very good line in *terribilità*, although it regularly worked against him. Building an opera house without a box office must rank him low on attention to detail, even though he applied himself assiduously to the most menial of tasks. Though his sons loved him, his team leadership was not good, because he seemed often to feel threatened by success in his employees.

The ultimate team leader was, of course, Christie, who also scores a hundred per cent for stubbornness, energy, and attention to detail. I am not sure how high he scores on optimism, since his financial standing was so secure that he never had to grapple with the possibility of failure on that account. His *terri-bilità* was undoubtedly crushing; yet since it knew no gradations and its outcome was invariably final, admitting of no appeal, and it was also utterly unpredictable, its usefulness to him as an impresario is questionable.

The quality that I would suggest as an additional ingredient necessary to successful impresario-ship is persuasiveness. This was a characteristic common to all three men, but is not to be confused with diplomacy, a synonym in this field for weakness, a buying of present peace at the price of future recriminations. When the singers are distraught, the creditors persistent, and the orchestra on strike, it is not compromise which ensures that the show goes on but persuasiveness, mixed with *terribilità*.

Acknowledgements

In re-telling the story of these three men, my principal debt has been to those authors whose own works are listed below. I have greatly relied on them, and their books are very well worth reading for the greater detail that they give. They have formed my principal sources, and without them this book could not have been compiled:

Dennis Arundell, *The Critic at the Opera* (Da Capo Press, 1980)

Wilfrid Blunt, *John Christie of Glyndebourne* (Bles, 1968)

Wallace Brockway & Herbert Weinstock, *The World of Opera* (Methuen, 1963)

Moran Caplat, *Dinghies to Divas* (Collins, 1985)

Hugh Carey, *Duet for Two Voices* (Cambridge University Press, 1979)

Humphrey Carpenter, *Benjamin Britten: A Biography* (Faber, 1993)

J. F. Cone, *Oscar Hammerstein's Manhattan Opera Company* (University of Oklahoma Press, 1966)

——*First Rival of the Metropolitan Opera* (Columbia University Press, 1983)

Edward J. Dent, *Opera* (Greenwood Press, 1979)

Frances Donaldson, *The Royal Opera House Covent Garden: In the Twentieth Century* (Weidenfeld & Nicolson, 1988)

Acknowledgements

Earl of Harewood, *Kobbé's Complete Opera Book* (Bodley Head, 1987)

Spike Hughes, *Glyndebourne: A History of the Festival Opera* (David & Charles, 1981)

Miles Jebb, ed., *The Diaries of Cynthia Gladwyn* (Constable, 1995)

Alan Jefferson, *Sir Thomas Beecham: A Centenary Tribute* (Macdonald & Jane's, 1979)

R. C. Latham & W. Matthews, eds., *The Diaries of Samuel Pepys* (Bell & Hyman, 1970–83), 11 vols.

James Mapleson, *My Memoirs* (Remington, 1888), 2 vols.

New Grove Dictionary of Opera (Macmillan Press, 1992)

Harold Rosenthal, ed., *The Mapleson Memoirs* (Putnam & Co., 1966)

Charles Santley, *Student and Singer* (Edward Arnold, 1892)

—— *Reminiscences of My Life* (Edward Arnold, 1909)

Vincent Sheean, *The Amazing Oscar Hammerstein* (Weidenfeld & Nicolson, 1956)

William C. Smith, *Italian Opera and Contemporary Ballet in London, 1789–1820* (Society for Theatre Research, 1955)

Eric Walter White, *The Rise of English Opera* (Da Capo Press, 1972)

Though it may seem invidious to single out any one author, John Cone's immensely impressive researches into both Mapleson's time in America and Oscar Hammerstein have been extensively mined by me, and are acknowledged with the most grateful thanks. In many cases he made clear what other sources left indistinct, not to say baffling.

I should also like to thank Sir George and Lady Christie, Betty and Lincoln Mason, Adele Mason, Adrian and Mijoko Thorpe, Lucy Tittmann, Bill Wellings; Caroline Knox, of John Murray, for her patience and support when this book ran into the sands of family life; Liz Robinson, who edited my text; and the unfailingly helpful and courteous staff of the London Library.

F.S.

Index